Open access edition supported by the National Endowment for the Humanities /
Andrew W. Mellon Foundation Humanities Open Book Program.

© 2019 Johns Hopkins University Press
Published 2019

Johns Hopkins University Press
2715 North Charles Street
Baltimore, Maryland 21218-4363
www.press.jhu.edu

T0310938

ISBN-13: 978-1-4214-3003-4 (open access)
ISBN-10: 1-4214-3003-7 (open access)

ISBN-13: 978-1-4214-3043-0 (pbk. : alk. paper)
ISBN-10: 1-4214-3043-6 (pbk. : alk. paper)

ISBN-13: 978-1-4214-3085-0 (electronic)
ISBN-10: 1-4214-3085-1 (electronic)

This page supersedes the copyright page included in the original publication of this work.

SCIENCE AND JUSTICE

The Massachusetts Witchcraft Trials

EXECUTION O

A. Hangman   B. Bellman   C. T

A

D

HES, A.D. 1655

nts   D. Witchfinder, taking his money

Sanford J. Fox

SCIENCE AND JUSTICE

The Massachusetts Witchcraft Trials

The Johns Hopkins Press, Baltimore

Lovingly dedicated to my wife

FOREWORD

Many years ago Justice Holmes urged that "we must beware of the pitfall of antiquarianism, and must remember that for our purposes our only interest in the past is for the light it throws upon the present." This wise man of law and life went on to say, "I look forward to a time when the part played by history in the explanation of dogma shall be very small, and instead of ingenious research we shall spend our energy on a study of the ends sought to be attained and the reasons for desiring them."[1]

However this may be, Professor Fox demonstrates that sound historical research can point to greatly needed improvement in the practical administration of justice and thus to the main ends of the law. His scholarly treatment of historical evidence is apparent throughout but is particularly well illustrated in the analysis of the defense of insanity (Chapter VIII). There, and notably also in the concluding chapter, the author shows meticulous care to distinguish facts from inferences and inferences from speculation.

Especially thought-provoking is the author's skillful diagnosis of the inadequate law-science relationship during the colonial witch trials. He points out that, while a few writings on law were occasionally consulted, no professional bar was involved in the witchcraft cases, this despite the "operation . . . of a legal system that in many respects showed sophistication and justice . . . in keeping with the best traditions of British due process." He demonstrates that "the administration of the law in the witchcraft

---

[1] O. W. Holmes, "The Path of the Law," Address delivered in 1897, *Harvard Law Review*, 10 (1897):474.

prosecutions was related in some rather complex ways to the world of science and scientists," and then, emphasizing a matter of great relevance to modern law reform, he concludes that "these constitute the framework within which some important contemporary problems may be clarified."

The author skillfully analyzes the religious, psychological, and cultural climate of colonial New England to account for the admixture of scientific and magical explanations of disease, not only by the Salem justices but also by physicians and midwives. In this connection he points out that, despite the anatomical and physiological discoveries in seventeenth-century Europe, there was a general belief that "*maleficium*, the harm produced by witches, was brought about by their manipulation of *natural* forces, so that the presence of naturally caused death was deemed perfectly consistent with the presence of witchcraft." In addition, "the institutional ability to deal with medical judgments openly and on their merits was wholly lacking," even though some of the magistrates were members of the Royal Society. "Their scientific involvement was, in short, irrelevant to their capacity to judge the quality of diagnostic evaluations."

While thus taking ample account of the cultural causes for the uneasy liaison between science and law in the witchcraft trials, Professor Fox concludes that "if justice involves bringing to bear in an informed way all that is relevant to the resolution of conflicts, then it must be said that it was injustice that characterized the use of science in the witchcraft controversy . . . for the reason that relevant and available scientific knowledge was either not used at all or was accepted *in toto* and put to indiscriminate use."

Have we made much progress since the witchcraft trials? The author answers this question in the negative. Despite the fact that we today "think we know more of what science really is and have assigned a learned profession to the caretaking of justice, there is still a discomforting similarity to the kind of injustice that obtained three centuries ago." It is true that patchwork improvements have been made, "yet all these advances leave more than a little to be desired. The ability of those charged with administering the law . . . to deal knowledgeably with scientific issues has not progressed very much beyond the days of the witchcraft trials. With full knowledge of the present and expanding importance of science in the legal process," the author justifiably chides, "we make no requirement that these professionals be anything but illiterates in science when they assume their responsibilities for the liberties, lives, and property of the populace." Bluntly and plainly, he concludes that "the legal profession has the responsibility and the opportunity to serve justice better than this, but it is grossly lacking in the knowledge and training it needs to do so." I have long held a similar view.

There is, however, hope for change. During the past two decades a few law professors have called for greater systematic and continuous liaison between the law and relevant paralegal disciplines; among these men has been Professor Fox, who, several years ago, in a persuasive argument emphasized the need for more effective cooperation between law and biology.[2]

There are, however, several matters to be observed in fruitfully guiding the emerging movement away from disciplinary parochialism toward a more just justice. First, in the law's pursuit of a more realistic justice, the stage must be set for systematic interdisciplinary training of lawyers, both initially and through refresher seminars and clinical participation. Second, adequate interdisciplinary texts must be developed for the new training.

Professor Fox has made a modest but noteworthy beginning toward achievement of the first desideratum. As a law teacher he is realizing in practice the need for interdisciplinary study in his classes on juvenile delinquency at the Boston College Law School; he is trying to have his students view legal goals in the light of the insights and promising potentials of psychiatry, psychology, and social casework.

But a great deal more remains to be done. I have long believed

[2] "Delinquency and Biology," *Miami Law Review*, 16 (1961):85–88, and "Legal Aspects of Biogenetic Crime," in *Biological Treatment of Mental Illness*, ed. Max Rinkel (New York: Page and Co., 1966), pp. 967–99.

that there is a need to establish a number of Legal Interdisciplinary Institutes at various universities, under the stimulus of farsighted law faculties. The objectives would be first, the assembling of authoritative materials in fields (among others relevant to the administration of justice) such as family life, delinquency and crime, racial relations, and labor problems; second, the working over of such materials by creative law professors, aided by specialists in various extralegal areas, with the aim of anticipating their probable relevance to major human and societal fields of future legislative and judicial concern; third, the dissemination of reports of such materials to judges, legislative reference bureaus, federal and state policy framers, and, in particular, to law school teachers and libraries.

Apart from its vital value as teaching material in the training of law students, the aim of an Interdisciplinary Institute would be to keep makers and interpreters of the law continuously informed of the progress of thought and experience in those fields of human endeavor with which legislators, judges, and administrators will probably have to deal in the not too distant future. At present, the reading by judges and other lawmakers in the fields of economics, sociology, political science, biology, and psychiatry tends to be rather sporadic and meager. About the only way in which significant research results on issues of business and labor, marriage and divorce, the protection of children, the relation of normal and morbid psychology to questions of criminal responsibility, and many other such problems find their way into the judicial mind is through the occasional exceptional briefs of counsel. But this method has the disadvantage of being drawn upon only as the occasion for litigation arises; it is not *anticipatory* of problems about to arise. Further, since briefs are constructed in the heat of litigation, they are likely to be less thorough, and certainly more partisan, than analyses of objective researches motivated not by particular lawsuits but solely by the search for the facts and their possible implications for future legislation and judicial decision.

As to the education of future lawyers, it needs to be emphasized that something much more fundamental is called for than the occasional tentative experiments in a few law schools. There is a crying need for a series of "West Points" of criminal justice, at which new generations of knowledgeable lawyers would be trained.[3] The proposed educational and training institution would be dedicated to raising the standards and vision of police officials, prosecutors, judges, correctional administrators, and others concerned with criminal justice.

It seems clear that the time has arrived for developing relevantly trained specialist criminal lawyers, or, in more general terms, specialists concerned with problems of law that affect persons more than property, who will dedicate themselves to the public service both in and out of office and whose range of interests will include all stages of the administration of criminal justice and related problems.

I confidently anticipate that Professor Fox will be an effective participant in the attempt to bring about the crying reforms needed in the legal profession. In the meantime, I am certain that the reader trained in law, the historian, the practitioner of various biological and sociological disciplines, and, indeed, the general reader will find his present work both scholarly and lively.

SHELDON GLUECK
Roscoe Pound Professor of Law Emeritus
Harvard University Law School

[3] Sheldon Glueck, "Law and the Stuff of Life," *Harvard Law School Bulletin*, 14 (1963):3–6. Bills to implement the idea are pending in the U.S. Senate and House of Representatives.

PREFACE

Why still another book on witchcraft, in view of the already vast amount of literature on that subject? To the historian for whom studies of the past require no extrinsic justification, the point should be made that the story of the trials is not retold here, nor are the individual tragedies redramatized. Rather, my attempt is to describe the part that science played in the prosecutions, examining first the aspects of science that were inherent in the Anglo-colonial conception of witchcraft and then the actual participation of scientists and awareness of scientific attitudes in the trials. In the light of this examination, it is clear that the witchcraft trials cannot be viewed as entirely, or even largely, the products of superstition and collective insanity. This book undertakes to show, in detail not found in earlier studies, that the investigations and trials were an integral part of the scientific ethos of the time.

In the field of legal history there has been no real attempt to trace the complex relations of the legal order with the scientific community of ideas and persons. It seems impossible to understand this neglect as reflecting a lack of things to describe and analyze. In the past three hundred years, the law could hardly have remained entirely aloof and immune from the ever-widening influence of science, and, in fact, it did not. Nonetheless, very little attention has as yet been directed to the historical interrelationship of law and science. Virtually the only aspects of this relationship that have attracted the interest of historians have been the legal problems engendered by the joint pressures of Enlightenment humanitarianism and the new psychiatry emanating from

France at the turn of the nineteenth century, and even in this area the effort has often been too limited and narrow; we are given, for example, merely descriptions of the villainous rejection by the lawyers of the virtuous doctrines propounded by the doctors. Deepening of our understanding of why law and psychiatry got along as they did still remains a task for the historians.

There are, of course, necessary limits to any historical study, imposed by the focus that is adopted, and dealing with the scientific aspects of the Massachusetts witchcraft cases has entailed making many exclusions. Inquiries such as why the 1690's saw such a proliferation of prosecutions and what effect these cases ultimately had on the law and the community have not been made, not because they lack historical significance but only because they lie beyond the scope of this particular study.

I must also acknowledge that this book has been written with an ulterior purpose: it represents a deliberate effort to shed some light from out of the past on some important current problems in the area of law and science. In that sense it is not "pure" history but seeks to communicate with those whose primary interest is in the proper administration of our system of justice. While much scholarship is now being brought to bear on the problem of the law's use and misuse of science, there is a noticeable lack of application of the wisdom of history, which this book attempts to remedy. My hope is that it will provide food for thought to lawyers and scientists in shouldering the responsibility they must share for designing and operating a jurisprudence that is modern, informed, and just.

My intellectual indebtedness in the preparation of this book has been formidable. The historical sense and sensibility of my wife have been a continuous and enriching resource. To my friend and teacher, Sheldon Glueck, is due more appreciation than can be briefly expressed here for his wisdom, guidance, and generous concern during its preparation. The students who have enthusiastically assisted in the work are, unfortunately, too numerous for individual mention. The secretarial help of Mrs. Mildred Lechiaro was invaluable throughout the course of the research and writing of this book. Stephen Morrison, Librarian of the Boston College Law School, and his staff—in particular Miss Herta Varenais— have provided indispensable, efficient, and gracious assistance in locating and obtaining works with which law librarians are not usually called upon to deal. The staffs of two other libraries, the Medical Library of Harvard University (now the Countway Library) and the Wellcome Library on the History of Medicine, London, have also been extremely helpful in the conduct of research by one initially unfamiliar with their resources.

S. J. F.

Boston College Law School

CONTENTS

SCIENCE AND JUSTICE

The Massachusetts Witchcraft Trials

I

A CASE STUDY IN LAW AND SCIENCE

✠

The history of science is still a new enough subject for the opening pages in such a work often to be devoted to supplying some reason why it should be studied or written about.[1] Even when this question has been settled, however, there is another level of controversy over whether a writer without professional credentials in a specific field of science has the competence to delve into its history or to comment on its social meaning. Here an affirmative and permissive consensus seems to prevail, so that under the leadership of such outstanding scholars as Arthur Schlesinger, Sr., and Jacques Barzun[2] it is not only those who "do" science who write about it usefully.

Perhaps these matters have been discussed so frequently and fully that the need for any further explanation of what follows in this book is obviated. Yet I do feel that something of the significance of the relationship between law and science must be suggested before the justification for examining a portion of its history can be assumed. This task is neither difficult nor lengthy. Law, as much as any other contemporary social institution, is deeply affected by the rules, discoveries, and ethics of modern

[1] See, e.g., A. Rupert Hall, *The Scientific Revolution, 1500–1800*, 2d ed. (Boston: Beacon Press, 1966), pp. 1–6.

[2] See A. Hunter Dupree, "The History of American Science—a Field Finds Itself," *American Historical Review*, 71 (1966):863–74.

science. The scientific ethos that permeates our culture makes a variety of interrelated demands upon law. First, an outright conflict between what is accepted as truth or reality in science and what is promulgated as truth or fact in law must be avoided. Such a clash would stigmatize the profession of law as unscientific and invite a degree of public disrespect and disrepute that could undermine the whole legal order. Second, relations between legal institutions and personnel and their scientific counterparts need to be, if not intimate, at least superficially cordial. If a significant segment of the scientific community shuns courts, lawyers, and the like with visible disdain, then regardless of the merits of any particular antagonism, the administration of justice becomes negatively valued, even to the point of affecting the self-esteem of the legal community itself. One factor impeding the recruitment of lawyers to the practice of criminal law has undoubtedly been a reluctance to join the ranks of those whose professional practice and theoretical heritage are scorned by leading scientific citizens of the community. Finally, science is a constantly changing body of thoughts and habits, demanding from law a structure capable of evaluating these changes so as to absorb, without undue delay, what has adequate promise of permanence, while at the same time withholding acceptance from the more ephemeral products of science.

With this background, then, one may well feel that what law does about science and scientists is important enough for us to examine a bit of relevant history. The witchcraft trials in colonial Massachusetts have been selected as the historical vehicle for a number of reasons. The leading consideration is that there was a substantial amount of science involved in the trials, in contradiction to the widely held belief that the whole matter was almost entirely an exercise in superstition, with a little psychopathology and back-biting thrown in. Both the preliminary investigations that took place and the witchcraft trials themselves involved important judgments on questions within the domain of the scientific community of the day. Where death or disease was the criminal harm inflicted, heavy reliance was placed on the knowledge and skills of the medical profession in determining whether the offense of witchcraft was involved. Once this question had been settled, the law continued to draw on medical resources in its effort to identify the culprit. The field of forensic psychology is also unavoidably involved: problems are posed familiar enough to any contemporary criminologist but in a context that directs attention to the nature of the underlying issues. Throughout, these prosecutions raise a broad range of questions concerning the ability of the law—in its procedures, concepts, and personnel—to exploit fully the knowledge and experience of the specialists it called on and, more important, to understand and take account of their shortcomings as well. A detailed discussion of this question has been reserved for the last chapter.

Seventeenth-century witchcraft is propitious for this inquiry for the additional reason that in that century the scientific revolution grew and blossomed. More than anything else, this revolution represented a fundamental change in the minds of men, a new orientation that involved pursuing new questions rather than replacing old observations with new ones. No one discovered in this century, for example, that it was *not* the nature of an apple to seek repose on the earth, as Aristotle had suggested as the reason why the apple fell.

More basic than any specific discovery, and near the heart of what was happening in science, was Francis Bacon's attack on scholastic science and creation of a new scientific philosophy that attracted spirited followers, in the persons of the founders of the Royal Society.[3] It was the intellectual inducement to a new outlook and framework for science that was at the core of the scientific revolution. Its visible products were, of course, remarkable. We tend to think that the astoundingly rapid accumulation of knowledge taking place in the mid-twentieth century constitutes a unique advance in man's understanding and control of nature. But on the whole, this century is in the process of perfecting technology, which involves little fundamental change either in

[3] See Margery Purver, *The Royal Society: Concept and Creation* (London: Routledge and Kegan Paul, 1967).

3

knowledge or in orientation toward nature. In contrast, one historian has described the events of the period of the scientific revolution as outshining "everything since the rise of Christianity and reducing the Renaissance and Reformation to the rank of mere episodes, mere internal displacements within the system of medieval Christendom."[4]

The witchcraft cases in Massachusetts are among these leaps into new dimensions in human understanding. When the first witch was hanged in Boston, in 1648, Copernicus' *De revolutionibus* was one hundred years old and man was well into the process of finding new lodgings for himself in the universe after having been evicted from its center. Vesalius' *Fabrica*, which awakened the great interest in anatomy and human biology, was published in the same year, 1543. The destruction of Aristotelian physics accomplished by the work of Galileo was already a quarter of a century old by 1648. It was only twenty years prior to that hanging in Boston that William Harvey effectively demolished all ancient physiology with his demonstration of the circulation of the blood. Well before the famous Salem trials in 1692, Descartes had drawn from the discoveries of his age the theory of mechanically linked causes in human affairs, and his idea found its way even into the court procedures of the Salem cases. From the middle of the century on, societies were being formed in Europe whose members not only set the standards of scientific thought for ages to come but also formed a link between that thought and intellectual development in America. Finally, of course, mention must be made of Newton, whose unique genius served to establish once and for all the new perspectives on the universe and man's place in it. In view of these truly revolutionary intellectual and material advances, we are obliged to ask at the outset how an era of such monumental achievement could tolerate even the accusation and trial, much less the outright execution, of persons as witches.

It must not be thought that this query is misdirected to seventeenth-century Massachusetts. There was in the Colony a lively

[4] Herbert Butterfield, *The Origins of Modern Science*, rev. ed. (New York: Collier Books, 1962), p. 7.

interest in scientific goings on. Several persons corresponded regularly with leaders of the Royal Society in London.[5] Contributions to scientific knowledge were made in astronomy,[6] and, as far as medicine is concerned, "the evidence suggests that contemporary European theories were known in Boston throughout the seventeenth century."[7] In their own way the Puritans of New England, no less than the Quakers in Philadelphia, accepted fully the scientific advances that were circulating through their intellectual environment.[8] In a later chapter I shall attempt to reconcile this interest with their simultaneous pursuit of witches.

There are two more factors that support the selection of these particular events as an appropriate historical case study of law-science relations. One is the singular and intense religious quality of the Puritan leadership in the Bay Colony. Few outdid these

[5] See Raymond P. Stearns, "Colonial Fellows of the Royal Society of London, 1661–1788," *William and Mary Quarterly*, 3 (1946):208. The respect entertained in England for the New England scientific setting is attested to by a notation in the Dedication to vol. 40 of the *Transactions of the Royal Society*. It states that Governor Winthrop of Connecticut had often met with men of science when he visited England and had participated in planning the founding of the Royal Society. Dr. Mortimer, Secretary of the Royal Society, writes further in the Dedication that "had not the Civil Wars happily ended as they did, Mr. Boyle & Dr. Wilkins with several other learned men, would have left England, and, out of esteem for the most excellent and valuable Governor, John Winthrop the Younger, would have retired to his newborn Colony, and there have established that Society for Promoting Natural Knowledge, which these gentlemen had formed, as it were in embryo among themselves."

[6] Thomas Brattle, for example, was "a merchant, a mathematician, and an amateur astronomer whose contributions won him the gratitude of Sir Isaac Newton" (Perry Miller, *The New England Mind: From Colony to Province* [Boston: Beacon Press, 1961], p. 196). These latter achievements were comet observations in 1680 which were used in Newton's *Principia* (see Dirk J. Struik, *Yankee Science in the Making* [New York: Collier Books, 1962], p. 49).

[7] O. T. Beal and R. H. Shryock, *Cotton Mather* (Baltimore: Johns Hopkins, 1954), p. 31.

[8] It has been suggested that the most satisfactory explanation for Quaker scientific interest lies in their great concern with man's condition in this world and its progressive improvement through the control of nature. See Brooke Hindle, "The Quaker Background and Science in Colonial Philadelphia," *Isis*, 46 (1955):253. On a somewhat different theological basis, the Puritan ethic was also centrally involved with man in this world. Some aspects of Puritan beliefs served to quicken the interest in scientific works, such as the faith that God had created a universe that was entirely ordered and therefore inviting and hospitable to investigation (see Perry Miller, *The New England Mind: The Seventeenth Century* [Boston: Beacon Press, 1961], pp. 207–35).

settlers in zeal and piety; they have in fact been called the "Left Wing" of Protestantism.[9] Their entire enterprise was devoted to the founding of a godly commonwealth that would provide an example for all the world to see and emulate. No part of the effort, including the system of criminal justice, could be permitted to escape its obligation to contribute to this end, at least that is the way the settlers felt at first. We will observe that later the very success they achieved in establishing a viable, independent, and prosperous society tended to erode their sense of identity as a beacon to mankind and that this loss, in turn, affected their ability to evaluate the scientific issues in the witchcraft cases.

A further argument in favor of the selection of this case study is the unusual autonomy the colonial leaders assumed in the sphere of lawmaking. Fairly early in their new experience the alacrity with which they chose to ignore restrictions on their civil power became manifest. Governor Winthrop relates that the General Court went so far as to declare that "our allegiance binds us not to the laws of England any longer than while we live in England, for the laws of the parliament of England reach no further, nor do the king's writs under the great seal go any further";[10] that was in 1646. More than forty years later it was clear how much this belief had become part of New England thinking. In response to one of the earliest colonial assertions of "the rights of Englishmen," the King's loyal judge, himself a product of the Colony, replied that the colonists "must not think the laws of England follow us to the ends of Earth."[11] Of course, this independence of speech did not indicate a desire to cut themselves off entirely from their legal traditions. It is plain that this would have been an impossible undertaking. The fact that several of the colonial leaders, including Winthrop, had served as justices of the peace in England served to ensure a large measure of continuity, since

[9] See George Rosen, "Left Wing Puritanism and Science," *Bulletin of the History of Medicine*, 15 (1944):375.

[10] Governor John Winthrop, Journal, in *History of New England, 1630–1649*, ed. James Kendall Hosmer, 2 vols. (New York: Barnes and Noble, 1908), 2:301.

[11] Quoted in Miller, *The New England Mind: From Colony to Province*, p. 156.

their experience with English law was a vital and consciously used resource in the construction of a new order. But given the necessity of observing the historical connection between one set of conditions and its neighbors in time, the legal institutions in Massachusetts and the administration of the witchcraft laws do represent a great effort to reflect dominant contemporary ideas and values. One result of this effort was the creation of a sophisticated and mature system of justice that not only carried forward English constitutional development but also anticipated by more than one hundred and fifty years major themes in American constitutional law.[12]

It would thus be a mistake to view the prosecutions as merely one aspect of a cruel, arbitrary, and retributive system of criminal justice. The evenhandedness of the legal system is demonstrated by much historical evidence. During the course of the century, for example, there were many more acquittals for witchcraft than there were convictions.[13] Moreover, the law did not jump in with a

[12] The literature of the legal system of early Massachusetts is large. A comprehensive discussion of the first two decades is found in George L. Haskins, *Law and Authority in Early Massachusetts* (New York: Macmillan, 1960). A recent description of criminal justice in the colony is Edwin Powers, *Crime and Punishment in Early Massachusetts, 1620–1692* (Boston: Beacon Press, 1966). In Appendix C, pp. 551–62, Powers compares the early Massachusetts statutes with civil rights and liberties today and cites the "due process" provision of the Body of Liberties (1641), which reads that "no mans life shall be taken away; no mans honour or good name shall be stayned; no mans person shall be arrested, restrained, banished, dismembered nor any wayes punished; no man shall be deprived of his wife or children; no mans goods or estate shall be taken away from him; nor any wayes indamaged under colour of Law or countenance of Authoritie unles it be by vertue or equity of some expresse law of the Country warranting the same established by a General Court sufficiently published" (Max Farrand, ed., *The Laws and Liberties of Massachusetts* [Cambridge, Mass.: Harvard University Press, 1929], p. 1). There is no question but that this rule of law was faithfully adhered to, even under the most trying circumstances. For example, the death penalty was withheld in the case of carnal knowledge of two girls under the age of ten on the grounds that the law was not sufficiently clear (see Powers, *Crime and Punishment in Early Massachusetts*, pp. 265–66).

[13] See, for example, the acquittal cases of John Godfrey (1669), in George Francis Bow, ed., *Records and Files of the Quarterly Court of Essex County*, 4:153; Mary Parsons, wife of Joseph Parsons (1675), in *Records of the Court of Assistants. Colony of the Massachusetts Bay 1630–1692* (Boston, 1901), 1:33; Hugh Parsons (1680), in *ibid.*, p. 189; James Fuller (1683), in *ibid.*, p. 228; Mary Webster (1683), in *ibid.*, p. 233; Mary Ingham (1676), in Nathaniel B. Shurtleff, ed., *Records of the Colony of New Plymouth in New England*, 12 vols. (Boston: William White, 1856), 5:223–24.

criminal charge each time the cry of "witch" was raised. It was not uncommon, for example, for a slander suit to be instituted by the witch against the "victim" of the purported witchcraft.[14] As to the severity of the law, it should be remembered that only fine and banishment followed a reference to the Church of Boston as "a whoare" and "a strumpet,"[15] and that the frequent resort in criminal punishments to public humiliation—the use of stocks and the wearing of signs—evinces a great concern for humbling the will of the offender as a means to his reformation.[16] There is, in fact, little that represents a community desire for pure retribution. The witchcraft cases in colonial Massachusetts, therefore, provide an opportunity to study the product of self-conscious and progressive lawmaking by a deeply ethical and religious people in an era of unparalleled scientific accomplishment.

[14] The testimony in one such case (1659) is preserved in detail in *Quarterly Court of Essex County*, 2:157–60.

[15] See the case of Francis Hutchinson, in Shurtleff, ed., *Records of the Governor and Company of the Massachusetts Bay in New England (1626–86)*, 5 vols. (Boston: William White, 1854), 1:109.

[16] See Haskins, *Law and Authority*, pp. 204–11.

II

THE ROOTS OF MASSACHUSETTS WITCHCRAFT

✛

One of the major shortcomings of much of the writing on Massachusetts witchcraft is that it concentrates exclusively on the events that arose out of the Salem trials in 1692. While in a strictly numerical sense these trials are the large bulk of the Massachusetts experience, a neglect of the preceding half century of similar events might imply that on matters scientific the Salem cases were basically different from the others. This is not so. In examining facets of the contributions of science and scientific attitudes to the prosecution process, it appears that there were striking similarities among the cases as they arose during the unfolding of the century. Thus we must take as our subject matter the entire range of largely homogeneous cases as they arose, from the earliest days of the settlement through the proceedings in Salem Village in the last decade of the century.

During this period, Puritan society was, of course, continually moving away from the strictly theocratic framework of its founders, and to some degree the aspects of witchcraft focused on here—in particular, the psychopathological concepts involved in the defense of insanity (discussed in Chapter VIII below)— reflect that process of change. But on the whole the developments within the society, despite their importance in other areas, were largely irrelevant to law administration as it affected witches, and the law's use of science remained constant. So, too, the cascading advances in particular areas of scientific knowledge made outside the Puritan community during the 1600's had no observable impact on the prosecutions: this sort of progress directly produced no changes in thought in the society that prosecuted witches that were sufficient to affect the prosecutions. Perhaps the age of science was an age in which attitudes toward science and nature changed, rather than an age of discoveries and inventions.

Even an examination of every witchcraft trial has its dangers, however. Such a broad span of time is still but a moment in the lives of people who were peculiarly conscious both of their past and their future. They valued equally their traditions and their ambitions, and their acts were flavored with a keen sense of their own position in world history. An aspect of this preoccupation—of great interest to us now—is the conception of witchcraft they felt had been passed on to them as an aspect of their political, religious, legal, and scientific heritages. These traditions, from which the Massachusetts cases spring, must be understood at the outset if what followed from them is to be seen in its proper light. Here the major focus of attention is on what meaning events and ideas had for a people at a given time and place in the past. More specifically, the fact that the mid-twentieth-century mind rejects magic and witchcraft as fanciful, superstitious, and perhaps even as a part of a delusional or psychotic outlook is of singular unimportance. It is possible that the set of beliefs that underlay the witch prosecutions may have been part of what has now been called "socially shared psychopathology."[1] But that is not likely, and to make the assertion stand that seventeenth-century Massachusetts was an insane society in this or other respects, a host of brilliant achievements in government, in theology, and in law, as well as a consistent course of ordered and reasoned reaction to the stresses of war, pestilence, and famine, must be explained away. Nothing short of a profound and unreasoning devotion to

[1] Ernest M. Gruenberg, "Socially Shared Psychopathology," in *Explorations in Social Psychiatry*, ed. Alexander H. Leighton, John A. Clausen, and Robert N. Wilson (New York: Basic Books, 1957), pp. 201–29.

the concept of monomania could maintain the belief that the witchcraft trials are simply manifestations of mental illness.

A look backward from Puritan times is therefore essential. In order to arrive at a reasonably clear view of the ideational heritage of witchcraft, it should first be pointed out that belief in witches appears to have been a universal phenomenon. It is, as George Kittredge has noted, "the common heritage of humanity. It is not chargeable to any particular time, or race or form of religion."[2] The discussion of the manner and rationale of scientific participation in the prosecutions which will follow should shed some light on the basis for this universality. But it does seem plain that acceptance of the reality of witches and witchcraft goes back at least as far as there are records to describe it. Henry Charles Lea, the historian of the Inquisition, wrote of sorcery and witchcraft within that context and was working on a detailed history of witchcraft when death deprived the world of his contribution to this field.[3] In his study of the Inquisition, Lea cites the case of the first known prosecution for witchcraft, which occurred in ancient Egypt in about 1300 B.C. Lea's account of the case reveals elements that will appear again millennia later, on the other side of the world. This is his description:

> The proceedings in the case recite, that a certain Penhaiben, a farm superintendent of cattle, when passing by chance the Khen, or hall in the royal palace where the rolls of mystic lore were kept, was seized with a desire to obtain access to their secrets for personal advantage. Procuring the assistance of a worker in stone named Atirma, he penetrated into the sacred recesses of the Khen and secured a book of dangerous formulas belonging to his master, Rameses III. Mastering their use, he soon was able to perform all the feats of the doctors of mysteries. He composed charms which, when carried into the royal palace, corrupted the

---

[2] George Lyman Kittredge, *Witchcraft in Old and New England* (Cambridge, Mass.: Harvard University Press, 1929), p. 372; Henry Charles Lea, *A History of the Inquisition of the Middle Ages*, 3 vols. (New York: Harper, 1888), 3:386.

[3] Arthur C. Howland edited a three-volume publication of Lea's last work under the title, *Materials towards a History of Witchcraft* (Philadelphia: University of Pennsylvania Press, 1939).

concubines of the pharaoh; he caused hatred between men, fascinated or tormented them, paralyzed their limbs, and in short, as the report of the tribunal states, "He sought and found the real way to execute off the abomination and all the wickedness that the heart conceived, and he performed them, with other great crimes, the horror of every god and goddess. Consequently, he has endured the great punishment, even unto death, which the divine writings say that he merited."[4]

What is noteworthy here is, first, that there is a firm belief that Penhaiben could and did in fact exercise supernatural powers of the sort described. There is no flavor of charlatanism or fraud even remotely implied; he "executed" the abominations. Second, there is no implication of impropriety about the use of these powers *per se*. Presumably, if Rameses III had done precisely what Penhaiben did, there would have been no abomination involved. The book must have been in the Khen for a purpose. To hypothesize further, the "doctors of mysteries" were privileged in the performance of these feats but did not use them for personal advantage. The accused was, in short, a magician without a license. This same prohibition on the *improper* use of magical powers seems to underlie the Exodus edict, "Thou shalt not suffer a witch to live," since the Old Testament is replete with instances of a *proper* alliance with spiritual powers for human purposes, for example, Moses producing water from a rock or Joshua commanding the sun and moon to stand still.[5] This emphasis on the matter of authorized vs. unauthorized sorcery did not end in Biblical days. As we shall see, the Massachusetts witchcraft cases also contain hints that the accused witches were engaging in practices—this time medical—that put them in unlawful competition with the colonial physicians. In view of the extent to which medical procedures of the day relied on astrology, alchemy, and other incursions into fields beyond human biology, the parallel with frank sorcery is apparent.

[4] Lea, *Inquisition*, 3:388. See also E. A. Wallis Budge, *Egyptian Magic* (London: Kegan Paul, 1899), p. 3.

[5] Exod. 17:6; Josh. 10:12, 13. The relation between Mosaic and Egyptian magic is discussed in Budge, *Egyptian Magic*, pp. 4–10.

If the belief in witches is the "heritage of humanity," it has been the peculiar heritage of the witches themselves that they be condemned and punished by those who wield secular and temporal power. Lea's collections of statutes and orders directed against them attest vividly to the fact that regardless of the stage of cultural development or the nature of the religious commitment that might be involved, societies have been virtually unanimous in their proscription of illegal magical practices.[6] Much of this opposition was generally based upon notions of good and evil, specifically, upon the alliance alleged to exist between the illicit magician and the forces of evil abroad in the universe, personified in Christianity by the Devil. The lines of battle were clearly drawn:

> As Satan's principal object in his warfare with God was to seduce human souls from their divine allegiance, he was ever ready with whatever temptation seemed most likely to effect his purpose. Some were to be won by physical indulgence . . . ; others by conferring on them powers enabling them apparently to forecast the future, to discover hidden things, to gratify enmity, and to acquire wealth, whether through forbidden arts or by the services of a familiar demon subject to their orders. As the neophyte in receiving baptism renounced the devil, his pomps and his angels, it was necessary for the Christian who desired an aid of Satan to renounce God. Moreover, as Satan when he tempted Christ offered him the kingdom of the earth in return for adoration, there naturally arose the idea that to obtain this aid it was necessary to render allegiance to the princes of hell. Thence came the idea, so fruitful in the development of sorcery, of compacts with Satan by which sorcerers became his slaves, binding themselves to do all the evil they could encompass and to win over as many converts as they could to follow their example. Thus, the sorcerer or witch was an enemy of all the human race as well as of God, the most efficient agent of hell in its empiternal conflict with heaven. His destruction, by any method, was therefore the plainest duty of man.[7]

[6] See Lea, *Materials*, 1:137–43, and *Inquisition*, 3:429–33.
[7] Lea, *Inquisition*, 3:385–86.

In spite of the directness of this injunction, it seems that the actual punishment of witches and sorcerers has had a somewhat checkered history. In the Roman Empire suppression was severe. With the opening of the Christian era vigorous action was taken against them, but this was all but completely abandoned in the period following the disintegration of the Roman Empire. The cycle of enforcement and neglect continued thereafter, evinced in penalties that range from the demand of ninth- and tenth-century continental legislation for mere penance for murder by sorcery to the penalty of death by burning for witches in the late Middle Ages.[8]

A variety of factors must have produced this ebb and flow in the severity of the penalties inflicted upon witches. It seems that the more secure the times—socially, politically, and economically —the less illicit incursions into spiritual mystery evoked official sanctions. But in the presence of widely felt turmoil and upheaval, the wrath of the state appeared in the form of energetic law enforcement. Probably the outstanding precipitating factor in Christian times was the threat posed by heresy. The connection between witchcraft and heresy is pointedly expressed in the above quotation from Lea. On the basis of this nexus one would expect the vigor of anti-heresy actions to be mirrored in the enforcement of the law against witches. Yet the persistent opposition to heresy did not always produce concomitant campaigns against witches; they enjoyed periods of relative peace during early heresy campaigns, probably because the express identification and merger of the concept of witchcraft with the idea of heresy apparently was not made until the Papal Inquisition of the Middle Ages.

While illicit magic had been condemned by the early Church, this prohibition was more in the interest of divesting the populace of pagan beliefs and practices in order to make room for the new Christianity and its ritual than it was an effort to preserve a Christian orthodoxy. The complex process of systematizing belief took centuries, and the refinements of the Schoolmen of the early

[8] *Ibid.*, pp. 392–425.

Middle Ages had to be developed before the opposite of this belief—heresy—could be definitively and systematically confronted. The anti-witchcraft and anti-heresy programs were thus parallel courses followed until the energies of the Church were fully mobilized in the period of the Inquisition, beginning with episcopal inquisitions conducted locally and progressing to the entire domination of the program by the popes and their emissaries. Significantly, this is also the profoundly unsettling period in the development of nation states and the breakup of feudal communities. But it was on the platform of clearing away heresy that the whole campaign of the next centuries was conducted.

Pope Alexander IV, in his bull of 1258, forbade the inquisitors to deal with magicians and required that these persons be left to the regular judges unless there was heresy clearly involved in their practices. This proviso in the bull, however, proved quite adequate as justification for the expansion of inquisitorial jurisdiction to sorcerers and witches. The reasons for this development are complex. Lea's explanation is that

> probably it may be traced to the effort of the theologians to prove that all superstitious practices were heretical in implying a tacit pact with Satan, as declared by the University of Paris. Thus, the innocent devices of the wise-women in culling simples, or in muttering charms, came to be regarded as implying demon-worship. When this conception once came to be firmly implanted in the minds of judges and inquisitors, it was inevitable that with the rack they should extort from their victims confessions in accordance with their expectations. Every new trial would add fresh embellishments to this, until at last there was built up a stupendous mass of facts which demonologists endeavored to reduce to a science for the guidance of tribunals.[9]

To this may be added Lynn Thorndike's suggestion that at these times the witch was the scapegoat for many of the ills of the waning medieval society and was more the victim of psychological and sociological pressures than of religious dogma. With this in

9 *Ibid.*, pp. 492–93.

mind, Thorndike warns that "it is possible to overemphasize the somewhat tenuous connexion between magic and heresy."[10] In the matter of moral responsibility for the prosecutions and actual causation of the executions, Thorndike is certainly correct in drawing into his discussion more than theology and the institutions of the Church. Witches were, after all, cruelly executed long before Christianity came into the world. But it is not witchcraft throughout time that we are here concerned with. In seeking to understand the roots of witchcraft in Massachusetts in the 1600's, it is vital to observe that there *was* a clear and observable "connexion" between magic and heresy on the continent which did not, for reasons to be developed, appear in New England, and the distinction was important in structuring the role of science in the Massachusetts cases.

During the course of almost four and a half centuries, more and more of the practice of the occult arts was assimilated into the conception of heresy. Pacts with Satan, illicit baptisms, unfounded assumptions concerning the Devil's power to act contrary to the will of God, and all manner of other acts came to be deemed a denial of the faith. An influential declaration by the Theology Faculty of the University of Paris in 1398 made virtually all such superstitious observances an error of faith.[11] Paris was the leading center of theological studies of the time, and thus a pattern was established that was widely and respectfully followed. The assimilation became so total that when Innocent VIII, in 1484, issued his bull authorizing the activity of two of the most famous inquisitors, Henry Kramer and James Sprenger (authors of the book for use in such cases, the *Malleus maleficarum*), he announced as his purpose the driving out of all "heretical depravity" and the desire that the "Catholic Faith should especially in this Our day increase and flourish."[12]

---

[10] Lynn Thorndike, "Magic, Witchcraft, Astrology and Alchemy," in *The Cambridge Medieval History* (Cambridge: University Press, 1936), 8:686.

[11] Lea, *Inquisition*, 3:464.

[12] The bull is printed in Montague Summers' translation of the *Malleus maleficarum* (London: John Rodker, 1928), p. xliii.

The significance of this statement is that, from this period on, witchcraft took on a new significance. Lea goes so far as to say that this was a "new witchcraft."[13] The emphasis on heresy considerations introduced a novel and important emphasis on the subjective elements of faith and belief. It was not that inquiry into observable secular harm was then abandoned—far from it. The second paragraph of Innocent's charter to the inquisitors contains a long list of "enormities and horrid offenses" committed by the heretical witches.[14] But as far as the ecclesiastical prosecution of witches was concerned, these abominations had only evidentiary value, and it was not necessary to prove the accused person guilty of such matters. Beliefs and errors of understanding being the central issues in adjudicating heresy, it was a confession that was the evidence most sought after. Thus, the *Malleus maleficarum* makes clear that if an accused is inconsistent in his statements to a judge, this is "sufficient grounds to warrant his exposure to the question and torture."[15] The fact that some punishment is authorized even without a confession is of no more than slight importance, since the availability of rack and screw rarely made it necessary to close a case without a confession.[16] The priests mention that "common justice demands that a witch should not be condemned to death unless she is convicted by her own confession,"[17] but the great emphasis on the abjuring of heresy found in the post-conviction procedures outlined in their

13 Lea, *Inquisition*, 3:493.
14 Summers, *Malleus maleficarum*.
15 *Ibid.*, p. 272.
16 The *Malleus* does call for an individualized use of torture (p. 273):

For some are so soft-hearted and feeble-minded that at the least torture they will confess anything, whether it be true or not. Others are so stubborn that, however much they are tortured, the truth is not to be had from them. There are others who, having been tortured before, are the better able to endure it a second time, since their arms have been accommodated to the stretchings and twistings involved; whereas the effect on others is to make them weaker so that they can the less easily endure torture. Others are bewitched, and make use of the fact in their torture, so that they will die before they will confess anything; for they become as it were, insensible to pain. Therefore there is need for much prudence in the matter of torture, and the greatest attention is to be given to the condition of the person who is to be tortured.

17 *Ibid.*, pp. 222–23.

handbook makes it certain that saving souls was a much more paramount consideration than procuring "common justice." To this end a penitent confession was an obvious necessity, and all other matters of proof and procedure derived their importance from their relationship to the procuring of it.

To the extent that the views represented in the *Malleus* characterized European witch trials, the above analysis would suggest that the relationship between magic and heresy was, in an absolute sense, a great deal more than tenuous. Once an accused witch was required by inquisitional procedures to respond to inquiries on items of faith, the matter of witchcraft became an incidental aspect of the heretic hunt. From a comparative point of view, however, the great importance of the heresy-witchcraft merger lies in the fact that the heresy factor did *not* play a significant role in the conception of witchcraft that was dominant in seventeenth-century Massachusetts. The central reason for this is that the turning point in the history of witchcraft, highlighted by Lea in his description of the extension of inquisitorial jurisdiction, seems to have had no analogue in English history: in England heresy never became the nub of witchcraft. Thus, the major source from which the Puritans drew their views in this respect was vitally different from the late stages of Continental witchcraft. To the English, and to the New England settlers, the essence of witchcraft was not belief or errors in faith but, as Kittredge puts it, "*maleficium*— the working of harm to the bodies and goods of one's neighbors by means of evil spirits or of strange powers derived from intercourse with such spirits."[18]

This interpretation of Massachusetts witchcraft requires amplification, since as late as the beginning of the fifteenth century witchcraft was a relatively minor problem in England. Pollock and Maitland mention but a handful of insignificant cases,[19] including several prosecutions that terminated in a jury acquittal. These events apparently led Lea to remark that "to the fair and

[18] Kittredge, *Witchcraft in Old and New England*, p. 24.

[19] Sir Frederick Pollock and Frederick William Maitland, *The History of English Law*, 2 vols. (New York: Little, Brown, 1895), 2:550–53.

open character of English law is doubtless to be attributed the comparative exemption of the island from the terror of sorcery."[20] Later, of course, England had a large number of witchcraft prosecutions, convictions, and executions. But of crucial importance to an understanding of both those trials and the Massachusetts experience are the facts first, that England was but little troubled by the problem of heresy and second, that the Papal Inquisition never took strong hold there.

The historians of English law Pollock and Maitland, in speaking of the crime of heresy, describe it as "an offense of which few Englishmen were guilty, and about which therefore our courts seldom spoke."[21] Lea mentions three known instances of heresy prosecutions in England in the early period after the Conquest, and adds, "but practically the orthodoxy of England was unsullied until the rise of Wickliffe."[22] But even the case involving heresy against the Lollards was largely a political problem, and Wycliffe's trial "ended in a scandalous fiasco."[23] Wycliffe himself died in peace, and it was not until more than twenty years after his death that a statute directed against heretics became part of English law.[24] It is, of course, possible that heresy was punished prior to this without a statute, a contingency disputed by Sir James Stephen on the ground that, if there had been some law against heresy earlier, it certainly would have been invoked against Wycliffe and his followers after the Pope and the Archbishop of Canterbury had declared their doctrines heretical and had even excommunicated some of them.[25] It seems that this matter of law enforcement against heretics "is a question that buzzes in a vacuum" by virtue of the paucity of pre-Lollard heresy in England.[26]

Just why England should have been so comparatively little

[20] Lea, *Inquisition*, 3:467.
[21] Pollock and Maitland, *English Law*, 2:543.
[22] Lea, *Inquisition*, 1:114.
[23] Charles William Chadwick Oman, "English History," *Encyclopaedia Britannica*, 11th ed.
[24] This is the famous *De haeretico comburendo*, 2 Henry 4, c. 14 (1400).
[25] Sir James Fitzjames Stephen, A *History of the Criminal Law of England*, 3 vols. (London: Macmillan, 1883), 2:443.
[26] Pollock and Maitland, *English Law*.

bothered with heresy is a fascinating problem, though one which cannot be explored here. But acceptance of the indications that this is so leads to the inference that English witchcraft probably did not trace the evolutionary path seen on the Continent. In the absence of a developing crisis in heresy, such as was experienced in Europe, there was relatively little reason for witchcraft conceptions to have focused on Devil worship and related actions from which the implication of rejection of religious orthodoxy could be drawn. Under these circumstances there is no reason to expect *maleficium* to be assigned a secondary role.

In the rest of Europe this heresy-connected focusing on subjective elements appears to have been brought about largely by the Inquisition, and therefore what experience the English had with the inquisitors is also of central importance. It was apparently quite limited, there being only one recorded instance of the Papal Inquisition operating in England. This related to the campaign against the Templars led by Pope Clement V. On November 22, 1304, Clement set off all the monarchs of Europe to hunt and try the Templars.[27] In the early fall of 1304, Edward II of England had expressed grave misgivings to other kings, even to Clement himself, as to whether there had in fact been any wrongdoing by the highly respected Templars. With the receipt of the bull of November 22, however, Edward initiated the required arrests and investigations. Compliance with royal orders was slow, and it was not until October, 1309, that the two papal inquisitors who had been sent to England to carry on the prosecutions were able to hold their examinations. To the surprise of the examiners, innocence was both stoutly asserted by the accused and warmly supported by most other witnesses. Worse still, the laws of England did not permit torture under ordinary circumstances, and further progress was thus stymied until, in mid-December, the King was induced to order the jailers to permit the clerical examiners to do with the bodies of the Templars what they pleased, "in accordance with ecclesiastical law." Even so, it was not until late May of the following year that confessions were finally obtained

---

[27] This was the bull *Pastoralis praeminentiae*. See Lea, *Inquisition*, 3:278–79.

from three of the Templars. Three months later, Clement protested to Edward and to all of the bishops of England that the reluctance to use torture in these cases was itself a serious offense against Church law. Thus prompted, in the succeeding year Edward stated again that ecclesiastical law was to govern the procedures used in the investigations by the inquisitors. Only in the last of his decrees on this subject, issued on April 28, 1311, did Edward actually use the word "torture." The ultimate outcome of this reluctant cooperation with the Inquisition was, as might be expected, but few convictions and, as punishment, merely a mild rebuke to the Templars for being defamed for heresy.[28]

From these episodes it appears that witchcraft in England had little association with heresy and consequently cannot be expected to have produced a strong emphasis on the subjective beliefs of the accused persons or on relationships established with Satan. To put the same thing affirmatively, Kittredge's contention that witchcraft presupposes some working of worldly harm seems acceptable in its application to the English experience. The basic heritage of the English *émigrés* to Massachusetts, therefore, was in "the trials of the Elizabethan age [which] did not involve acceptance, either by the people or by the judges . . . of the complicated and systematized doctrine which formed the basis for the inquisitorial proceedings on the continent."[29] The importance of this for our inquiry into the role of science in the colonial cases is that a fundamental issue in which science was frequently involved—the determination of *maleficium*—was a matter central to the whole undertaking and not a last-minute addition to the task of extirpating heterodox belief.

This discussion is not meant to serve as a complete description of the history of witchcraft in England, which is a complex (and fascinating) affair, involving political intrigues, the relatively slow process of Christianization, the influence of Protestant theologians who returned from exile in Europe upon the accession of Elizabeth I, and the persistent tensions between English monarchs

28 *Ibid.*, pp. 298–301.
29 Kittredge, *Witchcraft in Old and New England*, p. 24.

and the papacy. All of these factors have been well traced else-where.[30] The point being stressed here is that in spite of all the relationships between English and Continental experience observable in that history, English witchcraft remained an essentially secular offense.

There is no more interesting demonstration of the difference between the English and the Continental tradition than appears from a comparison of two virtually contemporaneous documents. Not only do they appear at about the same time but they also come from the same geographical area, and both issue from the pens of learned clergymen. One is a statement by Dutch and Flemish ministers in New York, written in October, 1692, in response to inquiries concerning the nature of witchcraft put to them by Joseph Dudley of Massachusetts. The other is from Cotton Mather and appears in his *Memorable Providences Relating to Witchcraft and Possessions* of 1689.

The New York clerics declared

> that the formal essence of witchcraft consists in an alliance with the Devil; that is to say, in that men (desert) the realm of God our Creator and Supreme King whom all are bound to obey in everything by reason of our dependence upon him, and whose glory everyone, to the extent of his ability, is bound to maintain against his enemies—and go over to the camp of the Devil in order to fight against God so as to increase and strengthen, as much as they can, the kingdom of the Devil. In return for this defection, the Devil, on his part, promises them his aid to gratify their lusts. Thus man, on one part, throws off the yoke of God bidding farewell to His precepts and promises, in order to belong wholly to the Devil, whom he holds in the place of God.

[30] See, e.g., Wallace Notestein, *A History of Witchcraft in England from 1558 to 1718* (New York: Russell & Russell, for the American Historical Association, 1911); C. L'Estrange Ewen, *Witch Hunting and Witch Trials: The Indictments for Witchcraft from the Records of 1373 Assizes Held for the Home Circuit A.D. 1559–1736* (London: Kegan Paul, 1929), pp. 1–47; Trevor Davies, *Four Centuries of Witch-Beliefs* (London: Methuen, 1947). The last cited work discusses the "rapid spread of continental witch-beliefs in England," but Davies obviously means by this the impetus to enforcement and not the alliance with heresy prosecutions (see his chap. 3).

Mather, on the other hand, defines witchcraft with a distinctly different and more worldly kind of problem in mind: "Witchcraft is the Doing of Strange (and for the most part Ill) Things by the help of evil Spirits, Covenanting with (and usually Representing of) the woful children of men. First, Witches are the Doers of Strange Things. They cannot indeed perform any proper Miracles; those are things to be done only by the Favorites and Embassadors of the LORD. . . . Secondly. They are not only strange things, but Ill Things that Witches are the Doers of."

By the close of the seventeenth century the problem of heresy had largely abated, but, nonetheless, the Continental tradition stands out clearly in the New York clergymen's description of the essence of witchcraft in anti-God, pro-Devil terms. There is, indeed, no mention at all of the problem of worldly harm. To Mather this is the nub of the whole question. Witches are, first and foremost, "Doers," and it is this view that characterizes Massachusetts witchcraft.[31]

English witchcraft cases also focused on the harm produced by witches; it was, in fact, a subject for complaint by George Gifford, writing there, in 1593. He declared that the law was imperfect in not punishing a witch proved to have had dealings with the Devil; proof of murder should not be needed to put her to death.[32] As will appear below, as far as formal legal provisions were concerned, Gifford underestimated the breadth of the proscription. He was quite right, however, regarding the actual administration of the law.

[31] The text of the New York clergymen, as well as the questions propounded to them, is found in *Proceedings of the Massachusetts Historical Society*, 2d series 1 (1884):348. Cotton Mather's description is taken from *Translation and Reprints from the Original Sources of European History*, vol. 3, no. 4 (1902):2.

[32] George Gifford, *A Dialogue concerning Witches and Witchcraft* (London: Reprinted by the Percy Society, 1842), p. 95. The same protest can be found in William Perkins, *A Discourse of the Damned Art of Witchcraft* (1608), discussed in Kittredge, *Witchcraft in Old and New England*, 290–93, esp. p. 292.

III

THE VIEWS OF SCIENTISTS

✠

As it is almost impossible for us today to conceive of someone's practicing magic and witchcraft, so we are impelled to believe that it must have been an equally difficult conception to maintain in any age in which scientific fact is given priority over unverified supposition and overt fantasy. How can we explain the fact that in the seventeenth century, the age of the great scientific revolution, which laid the foundations for the science and technology of our own times in virtually every field of knowledge, the belief in witches existed with such vigor that executions took place in New England into the very last decade of the century, or that the English statute against witches was only repealed in 1736? For an explanation it is simple and inviting to rely on the communication gap that then existed (and which has grown larger since) between science and scientists on the one hand and the rest of the population on the other. Witchcraft, in this sense, might be deemed the passion of the unlearned. But the troublesome fact is that it was not merely the non-scientific laity but the most eminent leaders of the scientific community that persisted in the belief.

This is not to say that there was always complete public unanimity on the subject. Dissenting views can be found, and indeed much of what we know of the lore of witchcraft is derived from writers engaged in the debate as active partisans. Not infrequently, in fact, modern discussion of this subject tends to divide historical characters into heroes and villains, the former, naturally, the contenders for disbelief and the latter the advocates of blind superstition. It is useful to look briefly at two such protagonists of the period because in their views the issues can be seen as they appeared to men of science and learning in those times.

The historians, by acclamation, have declared the outstanding hero to be John Weyer (1515–1588), a physician, who has been variously described as German or Dutch. Gregory Zilboorg has summarized his contributions to the field of psychiatry as follows:

> He was the first physician whose major interest turned toward mental diseases and thereby foreshadowed the formation of psychiatry as a medical specialty. He was the first clinical and the first descriptive psychiatrist to leave to succeeding generations a heritage which was accepted, developed, and perfected into an observational branch of medicine in a process which culminated in the great descriptive system of psychiatry formulated at the end of the nineteenth century. Weyer more than anyone else completed, or at least brought closer to completion, the process of divorcing medical psychology from theology and empirical knowledge of the human mind from the faith in the perfection of the human soul.[1]

Weyer did not hesitate to apply his talents to an attack on the practices of the Inquisition ("it is highly unpleasant to see how people, in order to kill errors, are busy killing human beings"[2]) and to the belief in witches that he found all around him. In a letter to his patron, Duke William of Julich, in 1562, he expressed the essential elements of his position on this subject:

> Of all misfortunes which the various fanatical and corrupt opinions, through Satan's help, have brought in our time to Christendom, not the smallest is that which under the name of witchcraft, is sown as a vicious seed. The people may be divided against themselves through their many disputes about the Scrip-

[1] *A History of Medical Psychology* (New York: W. W. Norton, 1941), p. 228.
[2] Quoted in *ibid.*, p. 209.

26

tures and church customs, while the old snake stirs the fire; still
no such great misfortune results from that as from the thereby
inspired opinion that childish old hags whom one calls witches
or sorcerers can do any harm to men and animals. Daily experience
teaches us what cursed apostasy, what friendship with the wicked
one, what hatred and strife, among fellow creatures, what dissen-
tion in city and in country, what numerous murders of innocent
people through the devil's wretched aid, such belief in the power
of witches brings forth. No one can more correctly judge about
these things than we physicians whose ears and hearts are being
constantly tortured by this superstition.[3]

It is difficult to ascertain the elements of thoroughgoing modern
science that Weyer has used to support his position. His attribution
of much of the misfortune to "Satan's help," to "the devil's
wretched aid," and to the machinations of the "old snake" seems
to preclude the assumption that Weyer refused to rely on supernatural interference in human affairs, which the role of pure
scientist would seem to imply. Zilboorg, who quite properly desig-
nates Weyer as a giant in the evolution of medical psychology,
insists that he did not himself believe in evil spirits and that his
references to the Devil are nothing more than the use of contemporary jargon to convey ideas about mental illness.[4] This may
well be so. The difficulty is that to his contemporaries these
references must have seemed to be a concession to prevailing
opinion that made his position both illogical and unpersuasive.
Dr. Meric Casaubon, for example, noted carefully that Weyer
admitted "no small part of what we drive at, when he doth
acknowledge *supernatural operations*, by Devils and Spirits."[5]
This led Casaubon to suspect Weyer himself of some illicit
trafficking with Satan and to suggest "that what he intended was
not so much to favor women, as the Devil himself, with whom
it is to be feared, that he was too well acquainted."[6] Weyer was

---

[3] Quoted in *ibid.*, pp. 213–14.

[4] *Ibid.*, p. 212.

[5] *A Treatise Proving Spirits, Witches and Supernatural Operations* (London:
Pawlet, 1672), p. 35.

[6] *Ibid.*, p. 46.

attempting to inject into the subject of witchcraft both the bene-
fits of his clinical experiences with mentally ill persons and a
heaping dose of common sense, but he lacked a structured philosophy of science into which his observations could be integrated.
More important, he failed even to begin to develop an epistemology that would relegate what was then unexplainable by science
to future scientific activity, as an alternative to accepting present
solutions from the non-scientific framework of theology. For, as
Wallace Notestein has observed, this framework was the real
point at issue: "Given a personal Devil who is constantly intriguing against the kingdom of God (and who would then have
dared deny such a premise?), grant that the Devil has Supernatural powers (and there were Scripture texts to prove it), and
it was but a short step to the belief in witches."[7]

No one illustrates the forcefulness of the argument developed
from these premises better than Joseph Glanvill. He was a Fellow
of the Royal Society and a determined advocate of the values of
the emerging science, yet he stands as the black villain in the
witchcraft controversy, as Weyer is the hero. His writing was
known to the Mathers in Massachusetts, and the Reverend John
Hale of Beverly, writing after the Salem trials, affirmed that
Glanvill "hath strongly proved the being of Witches."[8] Glanvill
noted that the dissensions produced by the Reformation had
promoted a growing theological skepticism, a process of disbelief
that might today be called "creeping atheism." Responsibility
for this state of affairs, he asserted, partly rested with those who
refused to accept orthodox views of witchcraft: "And those that
dare not bluntly say, there is NO GOD, Content themselves (for
a fair step, and Introduction) to deny there are SPIRITS, or

---

[7] A History of Witchcraft in England, p. 211.

[8] See Increase Mather's reference to Glanvill in his Remarkable Providences
(1684), reprinted in George Lincoln Burr, Narratives of the Witchcraft Cases
1648–1706 (New York: Barnes & Noble, 1952), p. 33. Cotton Mather's knowledge
of Glanvill is apparent in his Introduction to Memorable Providences Relating to
Witchcrafts and Possessions (1689), also reprinted in Burr, Narratives, p. 98.
Hale's reliance on Glanvill is indicated in his A Modest Inquiry into the Nature
of Witchcraft (1702), reprinted in Burr, Narratives, p. 405.

Witches."[9] Furthermore, he noted with authority, there was nothing in the new science that required such a blasphemous denial. Glanvill assigned to the mysteries of religion those areas of knowledge that science had not, and perhaps could not, appropriate to its own methodology and epistemology. It was to him of little consequence that religious doctrine could not explain just how the Devil and the witch go about their malevolent business. After all, he analogized, "we cannot conceive how the Foetus is formed in the Womb, nor as much as how a Plant springs from the Earth we tread on; we know not how our Souls move the body. . . ."[10] Mystery was no impediment to belief. Even that vigorous critic of much of the lore of witchcraft, Dr. John Webster, acknowledged that the Devil can make things invisible "by his spiritual power" and that the witch can accomplish strange deeds "by the strength of her imagination and the motion of her free will. . . ."[11] Webster, too, found murky metaphysics quite acceptable.

Glanvill's arguments were, if anything, more rigorous than those of Weyer. He recognized, for example, that the full force of history was on his side, and he exploited this advantage fully. The burden of proof he therefore assumed for himself was to demonstrate that it might be possible for witches to exist, not that there were, in fact, such persons. All of tradition declared the reality of witches, and, since the protesters asserted that this was absolute sham and untrue, Glanvill keenly undertook to destroy such arguments by proving the possibility of witchcraft: "If I show, how these things may be, and probably notwithstanding their allegations, though I say not down right that they are in the particular way I offer, yet 'tis enough for the design of Defense, though not for that of proof: for when one saith a thing cannot be, and I tell him how it may, though I hit not the

[9] *A Blow at Modern Sadducism In Some Philosophical Considerations About Witchcraft* (London: James Collins, 1668). The quotation is taken from the fourth edition, unnumbered page in the Preface immediately preceding p. B2.

[10] *Ibid.*, pp. 13–14.

[11] *The Displaying of Supposed Witchcraft* (1677), p. 252. On the title page Webster is identified as a "Practitioner of Physick."

just manner of it; I yet defeat the Objection against it, and make way for the evidence of the thing de Facto."[12]

As one might expect, the subtlety of Glanvill's distinction was frequently overlooked, for example, by Mr. Hale, in his assertion of Glanvill's proof quoted above. The proof that Glanvill did offer was based on appeals to many agencies of authority. In regard to religion, he declared that a denial of the reality of spirit, as distinct from matter, was a denial of God and of the soul.[13] He appealed to the concept of a Copernican universe where man loses his uniqueness and where creatures similar in spiritual quality to man might reside, beings who might be the agents with whom witches have their supernatural dealings: "And if both the superior and lower Continents of the universe have their inhabitants also, 'tis exceedingly improbable . . . that they are all of the meer sensible nature, but that there are at least some of the Rational, and Intellectual Orders. Which supposed, there is good foundation for the belief of Witches, and Apparitions; though the notion of a Spirit should prove as absurd, and un-philosophical, as I judge the denial of it."[14]

In addition, he suggested that common sense rebels at the thought that all of recorded experience with witches has been but one gigantic conspiracy and deception:

> And I think, those that can believe all Histories are Romances; that all the wiser would have agreed together to juggle mankind into a common belief of ungrounded fables; that the sound senses of multitudes together may deceive them, and Laws are built upon Chymera's; that the gravest and wisest Judges have been Murderers and the sagest persons Fools, or designing Imposters; I say, those that can believe this heap of absurdities, are even more credulous than those whose credulity they reprehend.[15]

There were, of course, others who entered the lists, and it seems fair to observe that the subject was controversial, at least

[12] *Modern Sadducism*, unnumbered page preceding p. B4.
[13] *Ibid.*, pp. 7–8.
[14] *Ibid.*, pp. 9–10.
[15] *Ibid.*, p. 6.

at a literary level. Reginald Scot, for example, denounced witch-craft beliefs in his *Discovery of Witchcraft* (1584), provoking the equally famous *Demonologie* of James I (1597). But Scot's refutation of witchcraft was deficient in much the same respect as was Weyer's. He granted the existence of evil spirits but failed to deal with the question of why they were not capable of produc-ing the malevolent system of evil known as witchcraft.[16] Another anti-witchcraft work that should be mentioned because it comes from a man with such attractive credentials is Dr. John Webster's *The Displaying of Supposed Witchcraft* (1677). Of Webster, Kittredge remarks that

> he was not exceptionally credulous, and he belonged to that advanced school of English physicians who, in the second half of the seventeenth century, upheld the general theories of Para-celsus and van Helmont in opposition to the outworn follies of the Galenists or regulars. He was a man of great erudition, of vast and varied experience, of uncommon mental gifts, and of pas-sionate devotion to the truth. I admire him, but I must be par-doned if I am unable to see how he can be regarded as a tower of skeptical strength in the great witchcraft controversy. Even his admissions on the subject of the fallen angels are enough to destroy the efficiency of his denial of current notions about witch-craft. Once grant, as Webster does, that our atmosphere is peopled by legions upon legions of evil angels, delighting in sin, eager to work mischief, inimical to God and man, furnished with stores of acquired knowledge, and able to devise wicked thoughts and put them into our minds, and it was idle to deny—in the face of the best philosophic and theological opinion of the ages—that these demonic beings can make actual covenants with witches or furnish them with the means of doing injury to their fellow creatures.[17]

We find, then, that skepticism and attempts to discuss the whole matter of witchcraft in terms of the thought patterns of science were ineffective because they failed to deal directly with the basic structure of good and evil in the universe and to assert

[16] See Kittredge, *Witchcraft in Old and New England*, pp. 340–43.
[17] *Ibid.*, pp. 348–49.

unequivocally the inability of evil forces to affect human affairs. Something needs to be said by way of explanation for this ineffectiveness.

The accommodation of the findings and views of scientists to the belief in witchcraft must be viewed as but part of their larger effort to preserve a harmonious relationship between religion and science. A major reorientation in thought was taking place in which priority was beginning to be assigned to knowledge gained from observation and experience rather than from the scholastically applauded channels of revelation and reason. Bacon's exhortations, at the beginning of the seventeenth century, that scientists eschew certain sources of what he considered to be misleading authority and embrace inductive techniques may have provided no precise methodology for actual scientific work; nonetheless, his powerful emphasis on induction furthered greatly the development of new, experimental, and fruitful means of learning the truth about nature. Clearly, an alternative to the truths of revelation was evolving.

There was also much in the world of science that was specifically threatening to traditional religious views, such as the findings and theories of astrophysics and astronomy, which destroyed for all time the anthropocentric view of the universe, a view that had become incorporated into dogma. The response of the scientific community to these and other dangers to religion was to assert that the study of nature, far from being a system competing in any way with the concepts of theology, was properly seen as an effort to advance further the proof of God and His works. Thus, Robert Boyle wrote that "for the sensible representation of God's attributes to be met with in the creatures, occurring almost everywhere to our observation, would very assiduously sollicit us to admire him, did we but rightly discern him in them. . . ."[18] There is probably no more thorough exposition of this view than Cotton Mather's *The Christian Philosopher* (1721), which provides a

[18] *Fifth Essay on the Usefulness of Natural Philosophy* (1663), quoted in Harold Fisch, "The Scientist as Priest: A Note on Robert Boyle's Natural Theology," *Isis*, 44 (1954):253.

sophisticated explication of the wonders of scientific findings as a means of demonstrating the genius of divine creation. Mather sees the body of man as "a Machine of a most astonishing Workmanship and Contrivance!"[19] He adds, "Yea, every Writer of Anatomy will offer enough to trample Atheism under foot."[20]

There was some objection made to this blending of science and religion whereby the former's major function was to prove the truth of the latter. Bacon, for example, recommended avoidance of "this unwholesome mixture of things human and divine [from which] there arises not only a fantastic philosophy but also an heretical religion."[21] Hobbes went quite a bit farther and demanded that only the data of natural science be accepted as the foundation of human knowledge, but he acquired few followers in this view. In view of the deep religious feeling of the age, it must have been perfectly plain to men of science that latent conflicts ought to be avoided and that "the way to advance the new learning was to insist upon its limitations."[22] Such a circumscribed role for science was, moreover, more than acceptable to the leadership of New England.

Puritan receptivity to the new science was encouraged, it seems clear, not half so much by the ocular proofs through which the new methodology was established as by the concomitant attestations of its theological orthodoxy advanced by its proponents. Particularly did the strategic line taken by the defenders of the Royal Society, by Boyle, Bishop Sprat, and Joseph Glanvill, insure Puritan confidence in the respectability of the movement. In order to avoid the accusation of atheism and materialism, in order to distinguish themselves from the Hobbesians, the Academicians put great stress upon their devotion to the spirit of "Scepsis Scientifica" and wrote energetically upon the vanity of Dogmatizing; as long as the conclusions of science could be deliberately advanced as tentative hypotheses, and as long as the scientists themselves were continually assuring laymen that more

[19] *The Christian Philosopher* (London: E. Matthews, 1721), p. 222.
[20] *Ibid.*, p. 223.
[21] Francis Bacon, *Novum organum*, pt. 1, sec. 65.
[22] Perry Miller, *The New England Mind: The Seventeenth Century*, p. 223.

remained to be investigated than had yet been studied, so that any impressions, garnered from our present imperfect knowledge, that seemed for the moment to challenge theological axioms would undoubtedly be corrected by future discoveries, then science contained no threat of heresy.[23]

At the heart of the matter is the fact that men of scientific learning accepted the basic theological framework of witchcraft, which made efforts at disputation by any of them largely futile. They found themselves at pains to demonstrate that their science did not pose any difficulties for religion, emphasizing that they did not know everything and that there were realms of knowledge and experience which were properly the exclusive domain of religion. But what is more important is that the belief in witchcraft followed from an unqualified acceptance of orthodox religious premises concerning good and evil and the potency of spiritual forces, and the rejection of this belief necessarily touched upon atheism. Science and scientists were therefore well advised to take care to avoid rending the fabric of belief in witchcraft. Any fundamental attack of this sort, express or implied, from scientific quarters would have been totally irreconcilable with the central effort to preserve the peace between religion and science. An authoritative condemnation of the belief in witchcraft as unscientific was neither present nor just around the corner.

This much of the discussion has been largely a matter of philosophy. Henceforth it will be concerned with how this philosophy affected the application of scientific knowledge and the use of scientific experts in the actual prosecution of persons accused of witchcraft. I turn now to a brief description of the legal system in which the prosecutions occurred.

[23] *Ibid.*, p. 222.

IV

THE LAW AND NATURE OF
MASSACHUSETTS WITCHCRAFT

✠

At the time of the colonization of New England, witchcraft was a statutory offense under the English law. Just how far back this crime can be directly traced is not clear. Although the *Leges Henrici* (*ca.* 1114) mention homicide by witchcraft as a capital crime, it was not until 1541 that a separate and distinct provision was made by Parliament for punishing witches.[1] In 1604 the final version of this law was enacted, the famous "witch act" of James I that remained on the statute books until 1736.[2] Both this law and its Elizabethan predecessor[3] contained separate provisions to cover the causing of death or bodily injury by witchcraft. They also proscribed the practice of witchcraft even without any resultant observable harm or *maleficium*. These latter provisions were directed at those who "use practice, or exercise invocations or conjurations of evil and wicked spirits to or for any intent or purpose."[4] Under both the 1562 and 1604 legislation these practices were punishable by death. There are, moreover, actual

---

[1] The first specific legislation, 33 Hen. 8, c. 8 (1541), was repealed by Edw. 6, c. 12 (1547). For a collection of pre-Norman, mostly ecclesiastical, laws, see Ewen, *Witch Hunting and Witch Trials*, pp. 2–4. There is a useful tabulation of the witchcraft acts from 1571 to 1736 in Ewen, p. 25.

[2] 1 Jac. 1, c. 12 (1604), repealed by 9 Geo. 2, c. 5 (1736).

[3] 5 Eliz., c. 16 (1562).

[4] This language is found in both the Elizabethan and Jacobean statutes.

prosecutions under both statutes for witchcraft of this "non-harm-producing" type.[5] In addition, the fact that in the law of James I death was the penalty for a first offense of bewitching a person without causing death is of some importance. Under the earlier statute of Elizabeth this non-fatal witchcraft was a capital crime only in cases of *second* offense. There were also more severe penalties under James for other aspects of witchcraft and sorcery, such as exhumation of corpses.

What these comparisons make clear is that, insofar as the statutory provisions were concerned, witchcraft without *maleficium* was not regarded as a minor offense and that, to some extent, the law in this area was becoming even more harsh under James I in the early years of the seventeenth century. The substance of the distinction made above between the English and Continental witchcraft cases is, therefore, not that there was no provision in English law for witchcraft of essentially a subjective or victimless nature, but rather that the kinds of prosecutions that were undertaken and their underlying theoretical basis in conceptions of heresy were much more characteristic of Continental experience with the Inquisition than of English. Kittredge's discussion of the English witch trials near the turn of the seventeenth century shows that the almost exclusive concern of law enforcement activity was with *maleficium*, as does Ewen's finding that in only 25 out of 202 convictions in the counties studied did the documents contain no mention of *maleficium*.[6]

In Massachusetts there was no body of written statutes before 1641, when the Body of Liberties was adopted after long discussion and debate.[7] In that compilation was included provision that

[5] See Kittredge, *Witchcraft in Old and New England*, pp. 282–86.

[6] See the full discussion of a typical case in Kittredge, *Witchcraft in Old and New England*, pp. 3–22, and his account of the pardons granted by James I to persons convicted of witchcraft, almost all of which did not involve *maleficium*, pp. 314–15. Ewen's list is in *Witch Hunting and Witch Trials*, pp. 102–8. But compare the argument that English witches were part of an illicit European religion in Margaret A. Murray, *The Witch-Cult in Western Europe* (Oxford: Clarendon Press, 1921).

[7] On this subject Governor Winthrop's diary notes: "This session continued three weeks and established 100 laws, which were called the Body of Liberties. They had

"If any man or woman be a witch, (that is hath or consulteth with a familiar spirit) they shall be put to death."[8] (The Laws and Liberties of 1649 reiterated this provision.[9]) The revocation of the charter in 1684 forced reliance on English law, and some of the 1692 Salem trial indictments therefore specifically mention the statute of James I.[10]

The phrasing of this colonial law presents some difficulty. On the face of it, it seems to limit witchcraft prosecutions to cases that do not involve manifest harm. The statute raises the question of whether the Puritans might not, in this respect, be drawing more upon a Calvinistic emphasis on notions of heresy than on the English tradition of requiring evidence of *maleficium*. There is some support for this suggestion in the fact that, while their English brethren left the punishment of heresy almost entirely in the hands of the ecclesiastical authorities, the colonists declared heresy to be a civil offense punishable by banishment, a sanction that fell little short of capital punishment in view of the Indian wars and the problems of survival in a wilderness.[11]

In spite of the restrictive language of the statute, however, the Massachusetts experience, like that in England, makes clear that the offense did encompass, and indeed was almost entirely limited to, the production of bodily harm and death by witchcraft. The first witch trial in Massachusetts, in fact, involved the charge that the accused had severely harmed her victims. Accord-

---

been composed by Mr. Nathaniel Ward, . . . and had been revised and altered by the court, and sent forth into every town to be further considered of, and now again in this court, they were revised, amended, and presented, and so established for three years, by that experience to have them fully amended and established to be perpetual" (Winthrop, Journal, pp. 48–49).

[8] The Body of Liberties is reproduced in William H. Witmore, ed., *The Colonial Laws of Massachusetts. Reprinted from the Edition of 1660, with supplements to 1672. Containing also, the Body of Liberties of 1641* (Boston: Published by the City Council, 1889). The declaration against witches is in Liberty 94, Capitall Laws, p. 55.

[9] See Winfield S. Nevins, *Witchcraft in Salem Village in 1692* (Salem, Mass.: Salem Press, 1916), pp. 29–30.

[10] See *The Laws and Liberties of Massachusetts*, p. 5; reprinted from the 1648 edition in the Henry E. Huntington Library.

[11] See George Lee Haskins, "Ecclesiastical Antecedents of Criminal Punishments in Early Massachusetts," *Proceedings of the Massachusetts Historical Society*, 72 (1957–60):21–35, esp. p. 24.

ing to Governor Winthrop, the witch, one Margaret Jones, "was found to have such a malignant touch as many persons, men, women, and children, whom she stroked or touched with any affection of displeasure, were taken with deafness, or vomiting or other violent pains or sickness."[12] She was hanged at Charlestown in 1648.[13] This was not the first execution of a witch in New England; we know, again on the authority of Winthrop's Journal, that some unnamed person "of Windsor was arraigned and executed at Hartford for a witch."[14] Burr says that this was Alse Young, hanged on May 26, 1647.[15] There are, however, no records at all concerning the facts of this earlier case. It is also clear that the parsimoniously worded Massachusetts statute was invoked as authority for charging death by witchcraft in 1680, for example. The indictment against Mary Hale in that year charged that she "by the abhorred sin and art of witchcraft did kill and bewitch Michael Smith to death."[16] She was found not guilty, however.[17]

It is impossible to examine in detail all the convictions for witchcraft that occurred in Massachusetts or in New England in the seventeenth century in order to determine the precise role of *maleficium*. In some instances, all that is known is that the case occurred. The conviction of the "woman of Windsor" (Alse Young?) is one example; the execution of the wife of Henry Lake of Dorchester[18] is another. The significance of *maleficium* in the New England and Massachusetts experiences must, therefore, be derived from interpolation. Prior to the Salem trials in 1692 and 1693, it seems that there had been five executions for witchcraft in Massachusetts and six in Connecticut. Of the Massachusetts witches, two, Mrs. Lake and Mrs. Kendall of Cambridge, are almost entirely unknown, with Mrs. Kendall only

[12] Journal, p. 344.
[13] *Ibid.*
[14] *Ibid.*, p. 323.
[15] Burr, *Narratives,* p. 408, n. 2.
[16] *Records of the Court of Assistants,* 1:188–89.
[17] *Ibid.*, p. 189.
[18] See Burr, *Narratives,* p. 408, n. 4.

briefly mentioned by the Reverend John Hale in his 1704 *Modest Inquiry*. It is significant, however, that Hale gives the charge as bewitching a child to death.[19] A third witch, Ann Hibbins, who was hanged in Boston in 1654, was the upper-class widow of a prosperous merchant and former Assistant of the Colony, as well as the sister of Richard Bellingham, one-time Governor of Massachusetts Bay. Of the charges made against her and of the record of the trial nothing remains. We do know that the jury found her guilty, a verdict which the judge refused to accept—which perhaps is an early example of differential treatment of accused persons based on socioeconomic considerations. Be that as it may, the case came before the General Court, where she was found guilty and sentenced to death.[20]

Of the three remaining Massachusetts cases, that of Margaret Jones has already been mentioned—Winthrop cites her having harmed other persons as the first of the charges against her. The next in chronological order, according to Poole[21] and Kittredge,[22] was that of Mary Parsons; it seems, however, that she was convicted and hanged in 1651 for the murder of her child rather than for any use of the black arts (this, at least, is what the official records state[23]). The last of the pre-Salem witches was Mrs. Glover, who was hanged for afflicting John Goodwin's children with violent fits.[24] Her case was made something of a *cause célèbre* by Cotton Mather's involvement in it, and we shall return to it later.

Thus, of the five Massachusetts cases in which the death penalty was invoked, the information available indicates that

[19] *Ibid.*, p. 409.

[20] This case does not appear in any of the official records. Nevins (*Salem Village*, p. 35) says that there is no trial record. The description in my text is from Thomas Hutchinson, *History of the Colony of Massachusetts Bay* (London: Thomas & John Fleet, 1764), p. 187; and William F. Poole, "Witchcraft in Boston," in *Memorial History of Boston*, ed. Justin Windsor (Boston: Ticknor and Co., 1881), 2:130.

[21] "Witchcraft in Boston," pp. 131–32, n. 20.

[22] *Witchcraft in Old and New England*, p. 367.

[23] *Records of the Governor and Company of the Massachusetts Bay*, 3:229. According to Nevins (*Salem Village*, p. 33, n. 9), Mrs. Parsons was reprieved and not executed.

[24] The case is described by Mather in *Memorable Providences*, pp. 89–131.

maleficium was involved in three (those of Jones, Kendall, and Glover) and was one of the major counts against these accused. In no case does there appear even a hint of a heresy charge, although heresy was itself almost a capital offense under the colonial code.[25] It would be somewhat surprising if the circumstances of the cases of Mrs. Lake or Mrs. Hibbins, now unknown to us, departed radically from this pattern.

The potential role of science in the determination of *maleficium* in the early cases seems, therefore, to have been of central importance. As to the Salem cases that occurred in the last decade of the century, the harm inflicted on the bodies of the tormented girls of Salem Village was the cause of the outbreak of prosecutions. There was, in addition, the charge that livestock had been bewitched;[26] Sarah Good, for example, was accused of bewitching seventeen sheep and hogs to death.[27] The well-known fits of the Salem girls were, moreover, not the only kind of *maleficium* the witches were supposed to have produced on the bodies of their neighbors. One victim complained of an infected foot from which was produced "several gallons of corruption" when lanced, and of sores in his groin "which brought him almost to death's door."[28] In only one of the 1692–1693 cases in which the death penalty was exacted—that of Samuel Wardwell, executed on September 22, 1692—does it appear that a significant part of the indictment involved the covenant with the Devil. It was charged of him that "about twenty years ago with the evill spiritt, the devill, a covenant did make wherein he promised to honor, worship and believe the devill."[29]

---

[25] *The Laws and Liberties of Massachusetts*, p. 24.

[26] The charge was made against Elizabeth How, who was convicted and executed (see Samuel G. Drake, ed., *The Witchcraft Delusion in New England* [Roxbury, Mass.: Woodward, 1866], 3:109, 111). She was also accused of bewitching a girl to death (see Nevins, *Salem Village*, p. 186).

[27] The victim was Benjamin Abbott; he testified against Martha Carrier, who was also convicted and executed. The testimony is described by Cotton Mather in *Memorable Providences*, p. 242.

[28] See Nevins, *Salem Village*, p. 56.

[29] Quoted in *ibid.*, p. 207. Wardwell was also charged with bewitching Martha Sprague (*ibid.*).

These Salem cases were tried after 1684, when the charter of the Colony was revoked, which placed laws such as the 1641 proscription against witches and its re-enactments in legal limbo. On December 14, 1692, the colonists enacted a new witchcraft statute that followed closely the text of the 1604 Act of James I.[30] The later indictments, such as that against Wardwell, specifically mention violation of the Act of James I. There is, however, no reason to assume that the adoption of the English act signified anything but an attempt on the part of the colonists to assure an independent political status for themselves through this demonstration of loyalty to English law.

A special court of Oyer and Terminar was appointed to deal with the witchcraft complaints emanating from Salem Village. The trials were of persons who had been first granted a preliminary hearing before a magistrate.[31] Earlier cases had all been heard before the regularly constituted courts, in accordance with generally applicable law. The trial of all capital cases took place before the Court of Assistants, composed of the Governor, the Deputy Governor, and the magistrates. In 1636 it was ordered that this court should hold four sessions annually at Boston.[32] In cases arising between these sessions the accused was bound over to appear before the next Great Quarterly Court, as the four sessions were called. In the cases before 1692 a grand jury indictment usually initiated the judicial process.[33] Imprisonment was generally the interim disposition in any event, since the law granting the right to bail did not extend to capital crimes.[34]

Provision was made in the law for carrying a case to the General Court when judge and jury could not agree on the verdict: "And if the Bench and Jurors shall so differ at any time about their verdict that either of them cannot proceed with peace of

---

[30] *Province Laws of Massachusetts* (Boston: Wright and Potter, 1869), 1:90. This statute was disallowed three years later (see Nevins, *Salem Village*, pp. 29–30).

[31] See Powers, *Crime and Punishment in Early Massachusetts*, pp. 469–73.

[32] *Records of the Governor and Company of the Massachusetts Bay*, 1:169.

[33] See, e.g., the indictment of Mrs. Joseph Parsons in *Records of the Court of Assistants*, 1:31.

[34] *The Laws and Liberties of Massachusetts*, p. 28.

conscience, the Case shall be referred to the General Court who shall take the question from both and determine it."[35]

Two witchcraft cases were processed accordingly, with quite different results. Hugh Parsons, husband of the Mary Parsons who had confessed to murdering her child in 1651, was convicted of witchcraft by the jury—a decision the magistrate could not accept. Upon a retrial in the General Court, he was acquitted.[36] As mentioned above, Ann Hibbins was convicted by a jury in the Court of Assistants, the verdict was refused by the judges, and the case was taken to the General Court. There, however, according to Thomas Hutchinson, "the popular clamor prevailed against her, and the miserable old woman was condemned and executed."[37]

One more point needs to be made concerning the efficiency with which the legal system operated. In the great majority of cases, the accusation of witchcraft and of relations with the Devil resulted not in a hanging or even a conviction, but in a dismissal of charges. The records show that before the Salem trials took place there were at least ten such dismissals, as compared with five possible executions at the most.[38] During the Salem prosecutions,

[35] *Ibid.*, p. 32.

[36] *Records of the Governor and Company of the Massachusetts Bay*, 3:273.

[37] *History of the Colony.* For a discussion of the general administration of criminal law in Massachusetts during these times, see Powers, *Crime and Punishment in Early Massachusetts*, pp. 424–54.

[38] Unice Cole was indicted for having familiarity with the Devil in 1662 and was found "not legally guilty according to indictment but just ground of vehement suspicion of her having familiarity with the devil" (*Records of the Court of Assistants*, 3:253–54). In 1673 the Court of Assistants dismissed the case against Anna Edmunds because "they saw no ground to fix any charge against her" (*ibid.*, 1:11). In 1651 Mrs. Hugh Parsons was acquitted of witchcraft (Nevins, *Salem Village*, p. 33, n. 9). Her husband, as noted above, was also set free. In 1674 Mrs. Joseph Parsons was found not guilty (*Records of the Court of Assistants*, 1:33). In 1665 John Godfrey was found not legally guilty (*ibid.*, 3:151). Mary Ingham was acquitted by a jury in 1677 (*Records of Plymouth*, 5:223). In 1680 Mary Hale was found not guilty (*Record of the Court of Assistants*, 1:189). A similar verdict was returned in 1683 in favor of Mary Webster (*ibid.*, p. 233). In the same year James Fuller was also acquitted (*ibid.*, p. 228).

Ewen (*Witch Hunting and Witch Trials*, p. 100) says that from 1558 to 1736 fully 78 out of every 100 persons charged with witchcraft in the five counties of the Home Circuit in England were not executed. Earlier (p. 31) he says that "the chance of a witch suffering the death penalty, when arraigned before the regular justice, was small, 81 persons out of every 100 escaping the rope."

twenty died, ten were condemned but not executed, and approximately ninety-six were never convicted.[39] It thus appears that there was much more involved in hanging a witch in Massachusetts than making the accusation. Proof was needed, and we must now turn to the role of science in providing that proof.

[39] The figures in the text are taken from Nevins, *Salem Village*, p. 254; Nevins gives "a partial list of persons accused whether convicted or not." There are 126 names on the list. The following names were omitted: 19 who were executed; Giles Corey, who was pressed to death for failure to plead; 8 who were convicted but released when the prosecutions ceased on September 22, 1693; and two who were convicted and died in prison—a total of 30. Volume 135 of the *Massachusetts Archives*, pp. 1–6, lists 91 names of persons accused of witchcraft from 1656 to 1750, including those executed. No attempt has been made to reconcile the Archives' list with Nevins'. The fact remains, however, that during the entire century, only a small minority of persons accused of witchcraft were convicted or executed.

V

MALEFICIUM AND CAUSE OF DEATH

✠

I t is difficult to say with certainty where a witchcraft case begins—
with a garrulous old woman, with an interpersonal relationship of
hostility and enmity, perhaps with an unexpected death. It would
not be surprising if in many cases a combination of these factors
produced the accusation. But whether it confronted the investiga-
tors initially or was encountered incidentally as part of the subsequent proof of a witchcraft charge, the issue of whether a
deceased met his end by natural means or by witchcraft was a
crucial one. In other words, the prosecution was obliged to prove
maleficium before a conviction could be obtained.

One obvious means of dealing with unexplained death, adopted
by the colonists in the early days of their settlement, was to conduct a coroner's inquest. As early as 1630, for example, a jury's
inquiry and view of a corpse resulted in a decision that a criminal
homicide had been committed.[1] The first codification of the laws,
in 1641, showed evidence of support for medical training in anatomy. This policy made possible the carrying out of post-mortem examinations, which might be extremely useful to such inquests.
It was implied in an exception made in the law governing disposition of certain corpses: "It is ordered by the Court that no
man condemned to dye shall be put to death within four days

[1] *Records of the Governor and Company of the Massachusetts Bay*, 1:77–78.

next after his condemnation, unless the Court see special cause to the contrary, or in case of martial law; nor shall the body of any man so put to death be unburied twelve hours unless it be in case of anatomy."[2]

Six years later, a more specific statement of policy appeared that put the General Court again on record in favor of developing the dissecting and anatomical skills of its medical personnel by permitting them to study cadavers systematically. It is sometimes suggested that enactment of this statute was caused by the need for anatomists created by the return to England of Giles Firman, Jr., who had taught anatomy during his stay in Massachusetts, from 1632 to 1677.[3] In 1677, discussing local medical education in a letter, John Clint wrote that "we never had but one Anatomy in the Country, which Mr. Giles Firman (now in England) did make and read upon very well."[4] Following Firman's departure the law declared: "We conceive it very necessary that such studies as physic, or chirurgery may be at liberty to reade anatomy and to anatomize once in four years some malefactor in case where be such."[5]

These statutes broaden the position taken in England as early as 1540, when Henry VIII's charter to the Guild of Barbers and Surgeons of London gave them the right to four bodies of criminals each year.[6] The Massachusetts colonists also brought with them the English experience with the use of coroners, and in

[2] *The Laws and Liberties of Massachusetts*, pp. 12–13. There is a strikingly similar provision in the Duke of York's laws, in force in Pennsylvania from 1676 to 1682, except that there is no provision "in case of anatomy." See J. B. Linn, ed., *Charter to William Penn, and Laws of the Province of Pennsylvania* (Philadelphia: George, Nead, and McCamant, 1879), p. 24. See also Frederick C. Waite, "The Development of Anatomical Laws in the States of New England," *New England Journal of Medicine*, 233 (1945):716.

[3] See, e.g., Timothy Leary, "The Massachusetts Medicological System," in *Methods and Problems of Medical Education*, 9th ser., vol. 9 (New York: Rockefeller Foundation, 1928), p. 303.

[4] Quoted in *ibid.*, p. 300.

[5] *Records of the Governor and Company of the Massachusetts Bay*, 2:201.

[6] 32 Hen. 8, c. 42 (1540). See William S. Copeman, *Doctors and Disease in Tudor Times* (London: William Dawson & Son, 1960), pp. 27, 40; Waite, "Anatomical Laws," pp. 716, 717.

1641 they enacted a law that "whensoever any person shall come to any very sodain, untimely or unnatural death, some Assistant or the Constable of that town shall forthewith summon a Jurie of twelve discreet men to inquire of the cause and manner of their death, who shall present a true verdict thereof, to some neer Assistant or to the next court (to be holden for that Shire) upon their oath."[7]

It is noteworthy that there is no mention of a physician's carrying out these responsibilities, as contrasted with the practice in colonial Maryland, where it is reported that "a chirurgeon often acted as the foreman of a coroner's jury."[8] There, the use of the expertise of medical persons is often quite clear, as in a Maryland case where the foreman of the coroner's jury, a chirurgeon, declared that the victim had met his end by means of a bullet "which entered the epigastrium near the navel on the right side, obliquely descending and piercing the guts, glancing on the last vertebra of the back, was lodged in the side of the ano."[9] There seems little room for doubt that full advantage was taken of someone's dissecting skill and anatomical knowledge in this case. The role of expertise is even more clear in another Maryland case in which the two physicians assigned to the corpse reported "that after they had cut open the body they found it clear of inward bruises, either upon the diaphragm, or within the ribs"; they added: "The lungs were of a livid bluish colour full of putrid ulcers, the liver not much putrid, although it seemed to be disaffected by reason of its pale wan colour: the purse of the heart was putrid and rotten, by which we gather that this person by course of nature could not have lived long, putrefaction being so near unto that noble part, the heart, even at the door."[10]

To what extent did allegations of death by witchcraft in Massachusetts involve similar examinations? It is important first to

---

[7] *The Laws and Liberties of Massachusetts*, p. 16.

[8] Raphael Semmes, *Crimes and Punishments in Early Maryland* (Baltimore: Johns Hopkins, 1938), p. 236.

[9] Quoted in *ibid.*, pp. 236–37.

[10] *Ibid.*, p. 237. Semmes provides several other examples of professionally conducted post-mortem examinations (see pp. 311–12, 238).

observe the use of medical skills in cause of death investigations generally. The records indicate that the coroner's inquest was used fairly often. As early as September, 1630, a jury reported that it had "vewed" a dead body and returned a verdict that "wee finde that the strookes given by Walter Palmer were occationally the means of the death of Austen Bratcher and soe to be manslaughter."[11]

A search for similar cause of death inquiries in the *Records of the Governor and Company of the Massachusetts Bay* (1678 to 1686), the *Records of the Court of Assistants* (1630 to 1692), the *Records of Plymouth* (1633 to 1691), the *Records of the Suffolk County Court* (1671 to 1680), and the *Records and Files of the Quarterly Court of Essex County* (1636 to 1683) revealed eighty-two such investigations. There were only two reports of murder, the great bulk (thirty-six) being findings of drowning. It is interesting that there were quite a few (twelve) suicides.[12] In only two of these cases, however, does there appear the hand of a medical man. In 1678, a jury report states: "Sir, according to your order, I with the rest of the men have searched the body of one called Edward. I made incision upon the parts of his body which was most suspicious which was upon the temporal muscle; I layed the bones bare: we could not find any fracture in the least, neither was the flesh in any wise corrupt or putrified."[13] The other medical report in the official records concerned the death of Jacob Goodale. In 1676 the jury, with the assistance of Dr. Zerobabel Endicot, made a post-mortem examination which indicated that Goodale had been beaten to death.[14]

[11] *Records of the Governor and Company of the Massachusetts Bay,* 1:78.

[12] The murder verdicts are in *ibid.,* 5:41, and in *Records of Plymouth,* 2:132. The drowning verdicts are in the *Quarterly Court of Essex County,* 2:119, 223; 4:98, 211, 212; 5:260, 444; 8:238–39, 442. They are also found in *Records of Plymouth,* 1:88; 2:151, 175; 3:15, 16, 28, 92, 93, 146–47, 158, 208–9; 4:83–84, 169, 170–71; 5:7, 94–95, 121–22, 123, 130–31, 141, 225–26, 262–63, 273; 6:8, 45, 75, 76. The suicide cases are in the *Quarterly Court of Essex County,* 2:421; 3:233; 5:124; 6:397. Also see *Records of Plymouth,* 3:213; 4:13, 83; 5:182, 208, 249–50, 262; 6:142.

[13] *Quarterly Court of Essex County,* 7:14.

[14] See the inquest report quoted in Francis R. Packard, *History of Medicine in the United States* (New York: Hoeber, 1931), 1:57. The trial of Giles Corey for inflicting the beating is in *Quarterly Court of Essex County,* 6:190.

John Winthrop reported two additional instances in which medical skills were used to determine the cause of death. In 1647 a surgeon who was called upon "to search the body" of the deceased found a fractured skull. This examination, however, did not take place until after the murderer had confessed.[15] Winthrop also cites a post-mortem finding of skull fracture in 1639 that led to a murder indictment.[16] Timothy Leary provides accounts of three more cases of post-mortem examination—in 1654, 1667, and 1674.[17]

In most of the cases that are known it appears that a gross view of the corpse was taken by laymen, their report typically concluding, "Wee, the said jury, having diligently serched him." When there were suspicious circumstances, the inquest sometimes resorted to what has been called the "ordeal by touch" or "bier right", an ancient practice based on the belief that when the guilty party touches the body blood will flow from the wounds or the corpse will in some other way indicate the identity of its slayer. Thus we find a Plymouth jury reporting that "further, wee required Anne Batson and seuerall of the family to touch the dead child but nothing thereby did appeer respecting its death."[18] John Winthrop's Journal mentions two other cases in which the touch of the murderer produced a flow of blood in the corpse, and Dow cites indications of this "ordeal by touch" being invoked as late as 1769.[19]

In only one instance does there appear a verdict of witchcraft returned by the jury. This was in New Hampshire in 1679, one year after it had become a royal colony. The setting in the town of Hampton is, however, clearly that of Puritan Massachusetts. According to Page, a jury of inquest viewed the body of a young

[15] John Winthrop, Journal, 2:318.
[16] Quoted in Packard, *History of Medicine in the United States*, p. 56, n. 14.
[17] "The Massachusetts Medicological System," p. 303.
[18] *Records of Plymouth*, 5:261–62.
[19] Pp. 218–19; George Francis Dow, *Every Day Life in the Massachusetts Bay Colony* (New York: The Society for the Preservation of New England Antiquities, 1935), pp. 203–4. This practice was not, of course, confined to Massachusetts. See Semmes, *Crimes and Punishments in Early Maryland*, pp. 126–27, n. 6; Harry B. Weiss and Grace M. Weiss, *An Introduction to Crime and Punishment in Colonial New Jersey* (Trenton, N.J.: Past Times Press, 1960), p. 47.

child and returned a verdict of "suspicion that the child had been murdered by witchcraft."[20] The jurors cited the appearance of the body to support their opinion, although they did not describe it. In addition, they relied on the odd appearance of the suspected witch and "the testimony that they heard."[21] There is no hint at all of the involvement of medical judgment.

In none of the other sources, however, is there a verdict that even alludes to witchcraft as being involved in the death. In Ewen's study of analogous records in England from 1559 to 1736, witchcraft is similarly absent. He reports: "One would have expected the coroners' rolls and inquisitions to be full of verdicts of death by witchcraft, but the writer has never seen any entry but felo de se, visitation of God, homicide, murder, or misfortune. Possibly, as in some of the gaol calendars, the word murder is used to include death by witchcraft."[22] In the two murder cases I found in the Massachusetts inquest reports, no concealment of witchcraft seems likely. In one, the murderer confessed to having used a knife and in the other, although the verdict did not identify the culprit, it did state that the corpse was "wounded in severall places, whereby, he was murthered."[23]

On the other side of this same coin is the fact that in none of the witchcraft trials does there appear to have been a coroner's inquest of any sort. The case against Rebecca Nurse, for example, included the charge of bewitching to death an eight-year-old child who had "strange and violent fitts for about two days and two nights, and then departed this life by a cruell and violent death."[24] A post-mortem inquiry, similar, perhaps, to the surgeon's search for "flesh in any wise, corrupt or putrified," as was mentioned in the 1678 Essex County report quoted above, might have revealed the cause of death. But none was done.

---

[20] Elwin L. Page, *Judicial Beginnings in New Hampshire 1640–1700* (Concord, N.H.: New Hampshire Historical Society, 1959), p. 118.

[21] *Ibid.*

[22] Ewen, *Witch Hunting and Witch Trials*, p. 60.

[23] *Records of the Governor and Company of the Massachusetts Bay*, 5:41.

[24] *The Historical Collections of the Topsfield Historical Society*, vol. 13 (Topsfield, Mass.: Published by the Society, 1908), p. 50.

We have, however, an autopsy report from Connecticut, dated March 31, 1662, which, although it did not result in an actual trial, sheds light on the present problem.[25] Elizabeth, the nine-year-old daughter of John Kelley of Hartford, died on March 26, 1662, after an illness of several days. During her sickness, Elizabeth complained several times that Goody Ayres was choking her and causing her other suffering. The same Goody Ayres seems to have been involved earlier with persons who were tried and executed as witches (Mr. and Mrs. Nathaniel Greensmith), but there is no record of any formal prosecution against her. A jury of inquest investigated Elizabeth's death and required Mrs. Ayres to touch the body, as a result of which the corpse "purged a little at the mouth." They also reported that "the backside of both the arms, from the elbow to the top of the shoulders were black and blue, as if they had been bruised or beaten." Five days after the death, on March 31, 1662, a physician named Bryan Rosseter, who had been summoned from Guilford, examined Elizabeth's body and reported as follows:

All these 6 particulars underwritten I judge preternatural: Upon the opening of John Kelley's child at the grave I observed,

1. The whole body, the musculous parts, nerves and joints were all pliable, without any stiffness or contraction, the gullet only excepted. Experience of dead bodies renders such symptoms unusual.

2. From the costal ribs to the bottom of the belly in the whole latitude of the womb, both the scarf skin and the whole skin with the enveloping or covering flesh had a deep blue tincture, when the inward part thereof was fresh, and the bowels under it in true order, without any discoverable peccancy to cause such an effect or symptom.

3. No quantity or appearance of blood was in either venter or cavity as belly or breast, but in the throat only at the very swallow, where was a large quantity as that part could well contain, both

<hr />

[25] The account of this case is taken from Charles J. Hoadly, "Some Early Post-Mortem Examinations in New England," *Proceedings of the Connecticut State Medical Society*, 69 (1892):207–17.

fresh and fluid, no way congealed or clodded, as it comes from a vein opened, that I stroke it out with my finger as water.

4. There was the appearance of pure fresh blood in the backside of the arm, affecting the skin as blood itself without bruising or congealing.

5. The bladder of gall was all broken and curded, without any tincture in the adjacent parts.

6. The gullet or swallow was contracted, like a hard fish bone, that hardly a pease could be forced through.

BR. ROSSETER.

Rosseter's report is of interest in several respects. For one thing, he opened the body "at the grave," indicating that Elizabeth was first buried and then disinterred for the autopsy. (It is not likely that the body would have remained unburied for five days or that Rosseter would have made his examination at the grave unless it was necessary.) Perhaps, therefore, his findings represent, in part, a failure to recognize as decomposition the changes that took place in the interval between death and the examination, i.e., a lack of experience with corpses after the *rigor mortis* stage.[26] Another point of note is that in only two of the six particulars does Rosseter expressly declare the findings to be to some extent beyond medical experience. The absence of *rigor mortis,* he says, is "unusual," and the discrepant nature of the skin and the underlying tissues and organs mentioned in his second particular is caused by no "discoverable peccancy" or corruption. The other four conditions are presented without any comment on his grounds for judging them to be "preternatural." Even in the first two, it should be observed that nothing expressly concerning witchcraft is reported. Rosseter finds the pliability of the body "unusual," but does not call it unknown or common in the case of witchcraft; he says the peccancy is not "discoverable," not that the symptoms have been induced from outside.

[26] See Theodore Shennan, *Post-Mortems and Morbid Anatomy,* 3d ed. (London: Arnold, 1935), p. 28. Rosseter also seems not to have understood post mortem lividity or gravity-induced settling of the blood in his findings 2 and 4 (see *ibid.,* pp. 23–24).

In short, Rosseter's report is almost entirely an objective description of his observations. He makes no mention of any sign or stigmata of a witch's intervention in the functioning of the body, such as impressions of fingers around the child's throat, etc. He stresses only what is novel or unexplainable to him, e.g., the blood in the back of the arms with no signs of bruising. Yet the central thrust of this medical report to laymen is that the morbid conditions he found were supernaturally induced, even those for which he knew there could be a natural cause. It is difficult to avoid suspecting that Rosseter's medical indictment of Goody Ayres was more the result of his embarking on his task in the belief that witchcraft had killed Elizabeth than it was the result of the autopsy findings themselves. Approximately six weeks after this report, there were court proceedings, apparently a preliminary examination of Goody Ayres on a charge of witchcraft. Undoubtedly, Rosseter's report played a significant role in bringing this action about. Since both Mr. and Mrs. Ayres fled from Connecticut, there is no record of a trial.

We have, then, a history of a not infrequent resort to post-mortems in cases of suspicious death; although there were no such investigations in the Massachusetts witchcraft cases, we are given some indication of what an autopsy report might be like where witchcraft was suspected. The attempt to account for the occurrence of any autopsies at all may provide a useful context in which to examine the witchcraft cases. There seems to have been no shortage of medical personnel to conduct these inquiries, in fact, the practice of medicine was a part-time occupation of many persons in the Colony. On the whole, these physicians were trained in a system of apprenticeship, and few had any medical schooling in the universities of Europe.[27] It was not until 1765 that the first American medical school opened in Philadelphia. During the seventeenth century, however, there were a number of doctors

---

[27] Carl Bridenbaugh, *Cities in the Wilderness*, 2d ed. (New York: Alfred A. Knopf, 1955), p. 447. See also Henry Sigerist, "Boerhaave's Influence upon American Medicine," in *Henry Sigerist on the History of Medicine*, ed. Felix Marti-Ibanez (New York: MD Publications, 1960), p. 202.

who were among the most prominent members of the community. Dr. Samuel Fuller of Plymouth and Dr. John Pratt of Cambridge, for example, were highly respected figures in the Colony.[28] There is, in addition, evidence that medical judgments were relied on strongly in other kinds of legal and semi-legal problems. In 1646 the court in Plymouth decided to allow one Francis Crooker to marry only if he could present a doctor's certificate that he was not an epileptic.[29] In 1651 Thomas Robinson was ordered to consult with physicians and to follow their advice concerning his impotence.[30]

On the other hand, the colonial experience with medicine was not entirely favorable. The regulation of quackery was no easy matter. Fines had to be levied to prevent the sale of medicines of no value.[31] The problem that arose in drawing a line between a permissible medical practice and the quackery that evoked public concern is nowhere more clearly stated than in the order of the General Court of May 3, 1649, regulating the use of novel therapies:

> Forasmuch as the lawe of God, Exod:20:13, allowes no man to touch the life or limme of any person except in a judicyall way, bee it hereby ordered and decreed, that no person or persons whatsoever that are employed about the bodies of men and women and children for preservation of life, or health, as physicians, chirurgians, midwives or others, shall presume to exercise to put forth any act contrary to the known rules of art, nor exercise any force, violence, or cruelty upon or towards the bodies of any, whether young or old, —no, not in the most difficult and desperate cases, —without the advice and consent of such as are skilfull in the same art, if such may be had, or at least of the wisest and gravest then present and consent, upon such punishment as the nature of the fact may deserve; which law is not intended to discourage any from a lawful use of their skill, but rather to encour-

---

[28] See Packard, *History of Medicine in the United States*, pp. 8–10; John Winthrop, Journal, 2:249.

[29] *Records of Plymouth*, 2:112.

[30] *Quarterly Court of Essex County*, 1:221.

[31] *Records of the Governor and Company of the Massachusetts Bay*, 1:83.

age and direct them in the right use thereof, and to inhibit and restrain the presumptious arrogance of such as through praesidence of their oune skill, or any other sinister respects, dare to bould to attempt to exercise any violence upon or towards the bodies of young or old, to the prejudice or hazard of the life or limme of men, women or children.[32]

Near the turn of the century, perhaps because this problem continued unabated, one university-trained physician in Boston declared the practice of medicine to be "perniciously bad."[33] Nonetheless, there does seem to have been a sufficiently large group of physicians for autopsies to have been undertaken in the witchcraft cases.

Apart from the matter of personnel, another set of factors to be considered are the fields of substantive knowledge involved in autopsy procedures. Foremost among these was anatomy. The scientific revolution had greatly increased knowledge of the human body, and these discoveries, in turn, might be expected to have stimulated medical men to work on cadavers. The new findings in science were manifested earliest in biology and human anatomy, although it is accurate to characterize the great scientific changes of the seventeenth century as primarily in the physical sciences, mostly in terrestrial and celestial physics. As was true in almost all of the divisions of human biology, the main sources of anatomical knowledge were the works of the great Roman physician of the second century, Claudius Galenus. In the centuries that stretched between his life and the dawn of modern times they had, of course, been added to and modified, but the doctrines that survived were clearly Galenic, perhaps even more than the central ideas in physics upon which Galileo worked were essentially Aristotelian.[34] In this sense, the changes in anatomy were more dramatically revolutionary than were those in physics.

Although not so intended at the time, the beginning of the

---

[32] *Ibid.*, 3:153.
[33] This was Dr. William Douglas. See *Massachusetts Historical Society Collections*, 2d ser., vol. 4 (Boston: John Eliot, 1816), p. 164.
[34] See A. Rupert Hall, *The Scientific Revolution*, pp. 77–92.

end of Galen's hold on men's minds may be dated 1543, the year in which Andreas Vesalius published his *De humani corporis fabrica* in Basel. This was a text based upon extensive practical experience in dissecting and was illustrated with an accuracy and wealth of detail earlier unknown. The *Fabrica* provided the fundamentals of knowledge that were to serve subsequent anatomists and medical men for centuries. However, it was not itself a rejection of Galen; indeed, when Vesalius found discrepancies between his own observations and the descriptions of Galen, he did not hesitate to conclude that Galen might be right.[35] Only infrequently did he state forthrightly that the traditional view was wrong.

Other anatomists followed Vesalius, some making quite significant advances in knowledge,[36] but relatively little of this knowledge had reached English medicine by the beginning of the seventeenth century. The commencement of English involvement in a new biology can probably first be seen when William Harvey announced his discovery of the circulation of the blood in 1628.[37] Largely because of this delay and the American system of apprenticeship training of medical practitioners, the early colonial period has been called almost entirely Galenic.[38]

Despite all the advances made in such areas as anatomy, circulation, respiration, etc., by pioneers such as Vesalius and Harvey, some commentators believe that there was remarkably little change in techniques of medical treatment or in the practice of medicine generally.[39] Even the latest publications in pathology, directly related to post-mortem anatomical findings, barely influenced the incidence or nature of autopsy procedures practiced by medical personnel.[40] The disinterest in anatomy, and perhaps in post-

[35] *Ibid.*, p. 139.
[36] See Charles Singer, *The Evolution of Anatomy* (London: Kegan Paul, 1925), pp. 135–74.
[37] See Kenneth D. Keele, *William Harvey* (London: Nelson, 1965).
[38] Maurice B. Gordon, *Aesculapius Comes to the Colonies* (Ventnor, N.J.: Ventnor, 1949), p. 3.
[39] Richard H. Shryock, *The History of Nursing* (Philadelphia: Saunders, 1959), pp. 134, 146–49.
[40] Seventeenth-century progress in this field is summarized in Esmond R. Long, *A History of Pathology* (New York: Dover, 1965), pp. 47–62.

mortem examinations as a consequence, is probably attributable, at least in part, to the distinction made between the functions of physicians and surgeons, whereby the latter group did almost all of the work we now associate with surgery. They also had a markedly lower social and professional status than the physicians, so that a reluctance on the part of physicians to engage in practice of a menial nature, as dissections and post-mortems may well have been considered, would be quite understandable. It is, in fact, one of the advances attributed to Vesalius that he himself cut up the cadaver in teaching anatomy to his classes, rather than simply lecturing on the parts as they were exposed to the students by an assistant, as was the tradition.

In the colonies the handicap created by the persistence of these traditional roles was aggravated by the fact that the apprenticeship system of educating colonial physicians was not well designed to keep the profession's recruits abreast of new developments in normal or morbid anatomy. Apprenticeship training emphasized the transmission of past knowledge and techniques, not the capacity or opportunity to assimilate novel ideas. Perhaps even if new doctors had been drawn from the English medical schools, this same negative result would have been produced. The fact that these developments in human biology came largely from individual scientists not associated with the established universities tended to insulate formal medical education as well from the changes.[41] To some extent, this was offset by the new means of communication established by the founding of the Royal Society in 1661 and the publication of its transactions. This was not without significance for the colonists. Governor John Winthrop of Connecticut was an original Fellow of the Society, although he was the only New England member elected in the seventeenth century.[42] We may infer, however, that others elected in the second decade of the following century (Cotton Mather, 1713; William Brattle, 1714; John Leverett, 1713; and Elihu Yale, 1717[43]) achieved that honor partly because of an interest in science that went back at

[41] Eric Nordenskiold, *The History of Biology* (New York: Tudor, 1928), p. 142.
[42] Stearns, "Colonial Fellows of the Royal Society of London," p. 222.
[43] *Ibid.*, pp. 226, 229, 230, 231.

least as far as the period of the Salem trials. Moreover, there was an active correspondence between eminent scientific members of the Society, such as Robert Boyle and Robert Hooke, and persons in New England.[44] Yet what stimulus might have been derived from the new knowledge was probably hardly felt by the bulk of practitioners. Shryock even suggests that conservative physicians were the chief obstacles to medical progress in the seventeenth century.[45] Thus, although there were probably enough physicians available for an expanded autopsy program that might have encompassed the witchcraft cases, their intellectual distance from dynamic developments in anatomy served to reinforce their traditional lack of interest in the new science.

In addition to anatomy, the physicians naturally drew upon broad theories of medicine and disease in their practice, and this, too, affected the scope of the cause of death investigations. The seventeenth century had inherited the humoral theory. The human body was believed to be made up of combinations of the four fundamental humors—blood, phlegm, yellow bile, and black bile. Health consisted of the proper mixtures and proportions of the humors; disease, even death, resulted from their imbalance or improper distribution. Unquestioning belief in such a theory made it pointless to conduct post-mortem examinations in cases evincing no obvious external traumata, such as would be caused by drowning or by a tree falling on the deceased. Without some understanding of the role of local pathology, doctors could usually hope to discover little of significance from a survey of the internal organs. Yet such examinations were sometimes done, so that we can see that this theory did not completely monopolize medical thought in the colonies or elsewhere. It is important to note that in the sixteenth century there were stirrings of new theories in what might be called chemical physiology, exemplified in the works of Paracelsus (1493–1541), Van Helmont (1578–1644), and the great English anatomist Thomas Willis (1621–1675). At about the same time, an explanation of bodily func-

[44] *Ibid.*, p. 220.
[45] *The History of Nursing*, p. 134.

tion, normal and morbid, was introduced that relied heavily on physical, especially mechanical, principles. This approach was developed in England and Scotland primarily by William Cole (1635–1716) and Archibald Pitcairne (1652–1713). But these ideas were not fully developed, influential, or adequately communicated to the bulk of medical men, at least until the impact of Cartesian and Newtonian mechanics came to be widely felt at the end of the century.[46] As one historian of medicine put it, "The medicine of the early seventeenth century presents no features to distinguish it from that of the preceding century. The practice and theory of medicine was mainly founded upon Hippocrates and Galen, with ever increasing additions from the chemical school."[47] During the course of the seventeenth century, the most significant movement in medical practice away from the dogmas of the ancients was toward a common-sense view that purported to scorn all theory. Perhaps the transitory nature of medicine in this era is best illustrated in the person of the famous English physician Thomas Sydenham (1624–1689), who rejected both the chemical explanations of his time and the humoral hypothesis of antiquity. He insisted that observation and reliance on the healing powers of nature were a safer guide to practice than resort to any abstract theory. Sydenham clearly understood that many diseases were caused by some kind of local pathology rather than by problems associated with the humors. Collaboration with his close friend John Locke, himself an accomplished physician, undoubtedly had an influence on the development of such an empiricism. In a letter Locke puts their view succinctly: "You cannot imagine how far a little observation carefully made by a man not tied up to the four humours (Galen), or sal, sulphur and mercury (Paracelsus), or to acid and alcali (Sylvius and Willis) which has of late prevailed, will carry a man in the curing of diseases though very stubborn and dangerous; and that with

[46] See Joseph F. Payne, "History of Medicine," in *Encyclopaedia Britannica*, 11th ed.

[47] *Ibid.*, p. 49; Shryock, "The History of Quantification in Medical Science," *Isis*, 52 (1961):220–26.

very little and common things, and almost no medicine at all."[48]

Thus, although significant work in pathology and morbid anatomy did not begin before the eighteenth century,[49] and progress in anatomy generally was out of the intellectual orbit of most colonial physicians, it may well have been an inquiring and developing empiricism that explains the limited number of autopsies that were in fact done in Massachusetts.[50] However, this interest in scientific investigation was not carried over into the matter of witchcraft. The administration of the law seems to have continued as though humoral theory were still unquestioned gospel. Still, the scientific community was not entirely unaware that some of the old medical dogmas were giving way and that its position on the power of witches could not remain completely static. It did face up to the necessity of reconciling its support of belief in witchcraft with the existing and expanding knowledge of the natural causes of death and disease. Its solution was to assert that the *maleficium*, the harm produced by witches, was brought about by their manipulation of *natural* forces, so that the presence of naturally caused death was deemed perfectly consistent with the presence of witchcraft. An expert scientific witness in one famous seventeenth-century English witchcraft case, Sir

[48] Quoted in *ibid.*, p. 50. See also David A. Givner, "Scientific Preconceptions in Locke's *Philosophy of Language*," *Journal of the History of Ideas*, 23 (1962):34; Patrick Romanell, "Some Medico-Philosophical Excerpts from the Mellon Collection of Locke's Papers," *ibid.*, 25 (1964):107. A close analysis of Sydenham's writing suggests both the presence of medical theory and something less than the thoroughgoing empiricism he believed he had adopted (see Kenneth Dewhurst, *Dr. Thomas Sydenham [1624–1689]: His Life and Original Writings* [London: Wellcome Library, 1966], pp. 60–67).

[49] Morgani's pioneering work, *The Seat and Causes of Diseases Investigated by Anatomy*, was published in 1700 and was translated into English in 1769. The first systematic treatise on morbid anatomy appeared in 1795, by Mathew Baille (see Payne, "History of Medicine," p. 52). Anatomical instruction from corpses was given for the first time in America in 1750 by Dr. Peter Middleton and Dr. John Bard in New York City. It was not too long before the public dramatically stated its opposition (see Jules C. Ladenheim, "The Doctors' Mob of 1788," *Journal of the History of Medicine*, 5 [1950]:23).

[50] See Sigerist, "Boerhaave's Influence upon American Medicine," p. 208. It is still true, however, that humoral theory was slow in dying out. As late as 1679, for example, Dr. John Barton of Massachusetts reported treating "an aching humor" by bloodletting (*Quarterly Court of Essex County*, 7:303).

Thomas Browne, summed up this position in his testimony relating to the fits suffered by certain of the witch's victims:

> And his opinion was, That the devil in such cases did work upon the bodies of men and women, upon a natural foundation, (that is) to stir up, and excite such humours super-abounding in their bodies to a great excess, whereby he did in an extraordinary manner afflict them with such distempers as their bodies were most subject to, as particularly appeared in these children; for he conceived that these swooning fits were natural, and nothing else but [what] they call the mother, but only heightened to a great excess by the subtility of the devil, co-operating with the malice of these which we term witches, at whose instance he doth these villanies.[51]

Browne spoke in terms of humoral doctrine, but the important point is that, no matter what *natural* causes of death an autopsy might reveal, the witch could still be held guilty for having brought about those causes. According to Cotton Mather, this English trial was "much considered" by the Massachusetts jurists.[52]

Such a view was affirmed by a man who attacked much in the traditions of witchcraft, Dr. John Webster. He declared that "what effects soever Devils or those called Witches do bring to pass in humane bodies are wrought by natural means, and proceed from natural causes."[53] To the inquiring mind, all of this leaves open the question of how natural causes can be thus supernaturally induced, a problem that did not escape the attention of Webster's contemporaries. After quoting at length the eminent physiologist Van Helmont as authority to show that the Devil did work by natural causes, Webster addressed the puzzle of the natural-supernatural nexus by asserting that the Devil can make things invisible "by his spiritual power" and that the witch "by the strength of her imagination and the motion of her free

---

[51] A Trial of Witches at the Assizes held at Bury St. Edmonds for the County of Suffolk: 17 Charles 2, A.D. 1665, in *Howell's State Trials*, 6:698.

[52] *Wonders of the Invisible World*, quoted in Kittredge, *Witchcraft in Old and New England*, p. 581, n. 16.

[53] *The Displaying of Supposed Witchcraft*, p. 247.

will . . . doth convey or inject these strange things into the bodies of those she would hurt or torment."[54] Joseph Glanvill, F.R.S., in defending the belief in the power of witches, grasped at essentially the same kind of explanation. He admitted that he did not know just *how* spirits did what they did. But, after all, "we cannot conceive how the Foetus is form'd in the womb, nor as much as how a Plant springs from the Earth we tread on; we know not how our Souls move the Body."[55] As a practical matter, Dr. Rosseter's report in Connecticut indicates that this difficult question need not be confronted. The autopsy surgeon need only describe the conditions he finds and then rely on the generally accepted belief that a witch could have produced them.

This constellation of ideas constitutes a perfect justification for neglecting post-mortem examinations where witchcraft was alleged or suspected. There was no post-mortem finding that could either confirm or deny the existence of the unknown forces suggested by Glanvill that were not within human understanding. In summary, it seems, that in spite of their distance in geography and in training from the locus of scientific progress in biology, the fetters of ancient doctrine did not prevent colonial medical men from engaging in some post-mortem examinations. When it came to witchcraft, however, this emancipation was quite irrelevant because the demonological theories propounded by them made evidence of witchly intervention wholly indistinguishable from their other findings.

[54] *Ibid.*, p. 252.
[55] *Modern Sadducism.*

VI

WITCHCRAFT AND DISEASE

✠

It will be recalled that the offense of witchcraft extended to *maleficium* short of death as it did to witchly homicide. The harm of this sort that a witch might inflict took a variety of forms. One victim testified, for example, that he felt "as if living creatures did run about every part of my body ready to tear me to pieces."[1] Another related that he had pains in his side and sores in his groin.[2] The victims of Margaret Jones, hanged in 1648, "were taken with deafness or vomitting or other violent pains or sickness."[3] And, of course, the physical suffering complained of by the girls in Salem Village is probably the best known instance of non-fatal *maleficium*. Even where death did result, there are cases where a pre-mortem investigation was made of the illness.

In the previous chapter the discussion largely centered around the absence of medical participation in the investigation of witchcraft. In the instances now being considered, where the victim still lived, the positive impact of medical science can be observed. Medical help was almost invariably sought to relieve the suffering, as it would be in any case of sickness. In the preliminary phase of

[1] This was the testimony of William Bradbury against Mary Perkins Bradbury, who was convicted in 1692 but not executed (Nevins, *Salem Village*, p. 212).

[2] Benjamin Abbott, testifying against Martha Carrier, executed in 1692 (*ibid.*, pp. 185–86).

[3] John Winthrop, Journal, 2:345.

the Salem incidents, for example, the Reverend John Hale reports that not only Doctor Griggs, but several other physicians as well, were consulted concerning the afflictions.[4] In an earlier case of suspected witchcraft, according to Cotton Mather, "skilful physicians were consulted for their help, and particularly, our worthy and prudent friend, Dr. Thomas Oakes."[5]

This was the common pattern. The colonists seem to have adhered quite closely to the injunction of Insitor and Sprenger in their *Malleus maleficarum* that the first test for the presence of witchcraft in these cases was the verdict of the physicians.[6]

The "verdict" that was forthcoming from the forensic scientists of the day was, however, not a simple one. Michael Dalton, an English writer of legal texts whose authority the settlers respected enough to have sent to England for two copies of his *Country Justice* as early as 1647,[7] dealt with the matter of the offense of witchcraft arising out of sickness of one sort or another: "Now to shew you farther, some signs to know, whether the sick party be bewitched. 1. When the healthful Body shall be suddenly taken, without probable reason, or natural cause appearing."[8] The first sign involves the diagnostic skill of the physician. Dalton appears to be saying that witchcraft is likely to be afoot when the illness lies beyond medical understanding—when a differential diagnosis rules out a natural cause. But immediately following his enumeration of signs, Dalton appends an important caveat, derived from Richard Bernard's *Guide to Grand Jury Men*: "But withal observe, with Mr. Bernard, cap. 2. that divers strange diseases may happen only from Natural causes, where he sheweth eight such several diseases; therefore, unless the Compact with the Devil be proved or evinced by evident marks or tokens . . . , it is not to be supposed that the Devil is the agent."[9]

Here is a skeptical view of the significance of "strange"

---

[4] *A Modest Inquiry*, p. 413.
[5] *Memorable Providences*, p. 101.
[6] Summers, *Malleus maleficarum*, p. 87.
[7] *Records of the Governor and Company of the Massachusetts Bay*, 2:212.
[8] Michael Dalton, *County Justice*, 4th ed. (London: John More, 1630), p. 274.
[9] *Ibid.*

diseases: they well may have hidden natural causes uninfluenced by witchcraft. In this warning Dalton reflected an opinion also held by some scientists, even by those who, like Dr. Meric Casaubon, were firm believers in witches. Dr. Casaubon's caution in this regard is especially significant because it is directed partly at what was then a poorly understood area of mental disorder ("melancholy") where ignorance—and hence a diagnosis of witchcraft—was highly likely:

> And indeed, that the denying of Witches, to them that content themselves in the search of truth with a superficial view, is a very plausible cause; it cannot be denied. For if anything in the world, (as we know all things in the world are) be liable to fraud, and imposture, and innocent mistake, through weakness and simplicity; this subject of Witches and Spirits is. . . . How ordinary is it to mistake natural melancholy (not to speak of other diseases) for a Devil? And how much, too frequently is both the disease increased, or made incurable; and the mistake confirmed, by many ignorant Ministers, who take every wild notion, or phansie, for a suggestion of the Devil? Whereas, in such a case it should be the care of wise friends, to apply themselves to the Physician of the body, and not to entertain the other, (I speak of natural melancholy) who probably may do more hurt, than good; but as the learned Naturalist doth allow and advise? Excellent is the advise and counsel in this kind, of the Author of the book de morbo Sacro attributed to Hippocrates, which I could wish all men were bound to read, before they take upon them to visit sick folks, that are troubled with melancholy disease.[10]

To what extent did medical men in Massachusetts observe these caveats advocated both by lawyer Dalton and physician Casaubon? The doctors did seem to have attempted to effect cures in the cases they attended, and it would be somewhat astonishing if they had not. Widow Carr, whose ailments helped to convict Mary Bradbury in 1692, was treated by Dr. Crosby.[11] Dr. Prescott attended the afflicted side, foot, and groin of Benjamin Abbott,

[10] *A Treatise Proving Spirits*, pp. 29–30.
[11] See n. 1 above.

whose testimony was instrumental in hanging Martha Carrier in 1692.[12] Dr. Fuller joined Dr. Crosby in treating Mrs. William Brown in 1669. The Browns testified against Susanna Martin in 1692 concerning this earlier bewitchment.[13]

In most cases we do not know the diagnosis upon which treatment was based, the nature of the treatment itself, or the course of the illness. But where this information does appear, it seems to be rationally related to both medical theory and the presenting symptoms. Thus, Dr. Prescott lanced Benjamin Abbott's sore, "from which several gallons of corruption did run out."[14] The Reverend Samuel Willard (1640–1707) described his experience with Elizabeth Knapp of Groton, who was apparently an hallucinating epileptic: "On the Sabboth the Physitian came, who judged a maine part of her distemper to be naturall, arising from the foulnesse of her stomacke, & corruptnesse of her blood, occasioning fumes in her braine, & strange fansyes; whereupon (in order to further tryall & administration) shee was removed home & the succeeding weeks shee tooke physicke & was not in such violence handled in her fits as before; but enjoyed an intermission & gave some hopes of recovery."[15]

This is full-blown humoral theory, and is a competent diagnosis for the times. But eight days later young Elizabeth "was again with violence . . . roaring, & yelling extreamly . . ."[16] Medical assistance was summoned once more: "The Physitian being then agen with her consented that the distemper was Diabolicall, [and] refused to administer . . ."[17] Elizabeth continued in this condition for several days, after which she regained some control and told

[12] See n. 2 above.

[13] See Drake, *The Witchcraft Delusion in New England*, 3:99.

[14] See n. 2 above.

[15] Willard's account, an enclosure to a letter to Increase Mather, is reproduced in S. A. Green, *Groton in the Witchcraft Times* (Cambridge, Mass.: J. Wilson & Son, 1883).The quote here is from p. 10. This Elizabeth Knapp is often confused with the woman of the same name who was executed as a witch in Connecticut in 1653 (see Drake, *Annals of Witchcraft* [Boston: W. E. Woodward, 1869], pp. 76–77).

[16] *Ibid.*, p. 11.

[17] *Ibid.*

Reverend Willard that she was bewitched. For reasons that Willard's note does not make clear, the accused woman was "by 2 evident and cleere mistakes . . . cleered."[18]

It is important to note that this pattern of attempting natural treatment and then, upon failure to arrest or reverse the condition, making diagnosis of diabolical intervention does not seem to be a uniform one. Concerning the afflicted girls in Mr. Parris' house at Salem, Reverend Hale reported several doctors in consultation but only one "gave his opinion, that they were under an Evil Hand."[19] Of this one, Dr. Greggs (or Gregg), it has been said that "he had expressed the same opinion of many of his patients when he could not understand their disease."[20] This was also true of Dr. Crosby, who told his patient he was "behaged"[21] and who, with Dr. Fuller, said that Mrs. Brown's fits were supernatural.[22] However, there is no indication that Dr. Prescott said that his patient, Benjamin Abbott, was bewitched, although Abbott was at times near death.[23] In Topsfield Joseph Ballard's wife was unsuccessfully treated by the local physician, but it was not until Ann Putnam arrived there from Salem Village that witchcraft was mentioned.[24] The doctor who was called in to treat the Putnams' child seems to have made no such diagnosis, even though "all he did give it could do it no good," and it died.[25] In some cases it is difficult even to know with certainty whether any treatment at all was attempted prior to the medical declaration of witchcraft. This question arises, for example, in connection with

[18] See Burr, *Narratives*, p. 23, n. 1.

[19] Quoted in *ibid.*, p. 413.

[20] Samuel P. Fowler, *An Account of the Life, Character, etc., of the Rev. Samuel Parris* (Salem, Mass.: Ives and Pease, 1857), p. 6. Fowler goes on to suggest that "it is highly probable that the opinion of these physicians went far to form the belief of not only Parris, but also of his ministerial friends, in the existence of witchcraft in the village. Mr. Parris appears to have been much astonished, when the physicians informed him, that his daughter and niece were, no doubt, under an evil hand" (*ibid.*).

[21] Quoted in Nevins, *Salem Village*, p. 212.

[22] Quoted in Drake, *The Witchcraft Delusion in New England*, 3:100.

[23] See n. 2 above.

[24] Nevins, *Salem Village*, p. 195.

[25] Deposition of John Putnam and Hannah Putnam v. Rebecca Nurse, *Historical Collections of the Topsfield Historical Society*, 13:50–51.

Cotton Mather's narration of the case against Mary Glover, who was executed in 1688. Mather states, concerning the illness of the victims, that one of the physicians "found himself so affronted by the Distempers of the children that he concluded nothing but an hellish Witchcraft could be the Original of these Maladies."[26]

There are a variety of factors that might account for the differing reactions of doctors to the baffling medical problems that confronted them in these cases. One that cannot be ignored is the variation in skill, experience and sophistication among the physicians involved. Kocher's evaluation of this problem in England may be equally applicable to the New England scene. There is, he suggests, a state of mind concomitant to sophisticated knowledge that is something in the nature of a belief that medical secrets still locked in mystery will some day yield to the accumulation of experience and experiment. The stronger this expectation of earthly progress, the more reluctant the practitioner will be to affirm that he faces supernatural forces in treating his patient.[27] On the other hand, those medical men with little awareness of medicine as an integral part of a culture's evolution will be more inclined to accept a fairly static state of knowledge and will resort more willingly to the notion of witchcraft.

However, this is only a partial explanation. The diversity of medical judgments is probably more directly related to the contemporaneous theology of medicine than to the professional sophistication of individual practitioners. Even among the most skilled there was likely to be a division of opinion that might well manifest itself in the witchcraft issue. The traditions of medicine affirmed that all human maladies, disease included, were traceable to God. It is true that in England, and probably in America too, there was a small number of atheistic, radical physicians who practiced within a completely materialistic framework.[28] But for

[26] *Memorable Providences*, p. 101. For similar ambiguities in reports of experience in England, see, e.g., Kittredge, *Witchcraft in Old and New England*, p. 302.

[27] Paul H. Kocher, *Science and Religion in Elizabethan England* (San Marino, Calif.: The Huntington Library, 1953), p. 142.

[28] *Ibid.*, p. 263. Weyer is somewhat affiliated with this group by virtue of his belief that "those illnesses the origin of which is attributable to witches come

the most part within the medical profession there were varying degrees of acceptance of the traditional view of divine causation. One position, taken by the less pious members of the group, was to acknowledge perfunctorily God as the ultimate cause but then to virtually ignore Him in an all-consuming concern for the natural forces that were deemed the proper business of medicine. Spiritual matters, if they played a part in a medical case at all, were entirely the domain of the clergy.[29] In this view is the seed of the modern attitude that distinguishes, with a high degree of mutual exclusiveness, the material and spiritual sides of man. In the seventeenth century such a position was likely to produce intense efforts at cure on the part of the physician and then, if the therapy failed, his passive acquiescence in witchcraft proceedings without any formal declaration by him that *maleficium* was present.

Considering the high incidence of sickness among the settlers, sometimes on an epidemic scale, and the relatively small number of witchcraft cases that arose, it seems fair to infer that most of the medical men in the colony kept their religious beliefs at a distance from their professional judgments, which thereby precluded their making a diagnosis of witchcraft when treatment failed. It is equally plain that a minority were involved in a mixture of piety and practice. Dr. Oakes, Dr. Fuller, and Dr. Greggs did not hesitate to use witchcraft as a diagnosis. Kittredge relates that in England even a man reputed "the greatest physician of his time" was first baffled by a patient's fits and then "ascribed the fits to witchcraft, remarking that he himself 'had some experience of the malice of some witches.' "[30] These men evince not a lack of

---

from natural causes" (quoted in Zilboorg, *A History of Medical Psychology*, p. 214). But, as has been discussed in Chapter III, Weyer's readers could quite properly take this as merely a description of his own experience, since he makes all the concessions concerning Satan and God that are necessary to support contrary assertions from the experience of others that witches can and do cause illness. His position is further undermined by the belief that the Devil works through natural means and that, therefore, a finding of natural causes does not preclude the possibility of evil interference.

[29] Kocher, *Elizabethan England*, pp. 264–65.
[30] *Witchcraft in Old and New England.*

medical skill—there are still a good many illnesses which might be described as "fits" that elude scientific mastery—so much as a belief that God's role in human affairs is not limited to the Creation, but that His intervention can be seen all through the course of life. God was seen as the cause of particular cases. In one's professional activity, therefore, one always had to be on the lookout for signs of supernatural forces.[31]

Perhaps the best representative of this latter group is Cotton Mather, whose emphasis on religion was accompanied by an extraordinary erudition in scientific affairs; he has, in fact, been called by one scholar the first significant figure in American medicine.[32] His willingness to draw a firm line on one side of which lies the impact of spirits is revealed in his description of John Goodwin's child, who was afflicted by witch Glover with "strange Fits, beyond those that attend an Epilepsy, or a Catalepsy, or those that they call the Diseases of Astonishment."[33] Mather had, of course, no doubts about the existence and power of witches and could in no way accept the implication of atheism that a denial of them would have entailed. Yet he devoured scientific literature[34] and as a consequence sought a rational way of resisting the materialism that the scientific progress he observed seemed more and more to imply. This he accomplished by postulating a *"Nismath Chaim"* (breath of life) as a vital principle that functioned somewhere between the immortal soul and the physical body.[35] The consequence of this was an imperative to go beyond mere physical factors, for "most certainly, the Physician that can find out Remedies . . . that shall have a more immediate Efficacy to brighten, and strengthen, and Comfort, the *Nismath Chaim*, will be the most successful Physician in the World."[36] It is but a small step from

[31] See Kocher, *Elizabethan England*, pp. 263–64. The printed records reveal only one instance in which a physician is alleged to have diagnosed witchcraft and yet no prosecution took place (see *Quarterly Court of Essex County*, 4:207).

[32] O. T. Beal, "Cotton Mather, the First Significant Figure in American Medicine," *Bulletin of the History of Medicine*, 26 (1952):103.

[33] Cotton Mather, *Memorable Providences*, p. 101.

[34] See Miller, *The New England Mind: From Colony to Province*, p. 345.

[35] See Beal and Shryock, *Cotton Mather*, pp. 67–68.

[36] Quoted from Mather's *The Angel of Bethesda*, in *ibid.*, p. 69.

the *Nismath* and its effects on health to acceptance of an active role of evil spirits in health and illness. A firm belief in such a God-centered vitalism needed only the addition of the common belief in witches to propel the frustrated physician into a diagnosis of witchcraft.

It is important to note that this insistence that spirit effects material events was not limited to clerical efforts to preserve the concept of the omnipotence of God. There was impressive scientific authority to support an attending physician who refused to limit his conception of the human body to its physical dimensions. William Harvey, for example, had demonstrated a materialistic and mechanical circulation of the blood in 1628. But in 1651 he wrote:

> The blood considered absolutely and by itself, without the veins, in so far as it is an elementary fluid, and composed of several parts . . . possesses but few, and these not very obvious virtues. Contained within the veins, however, inasmuch as it is an integral part of the body, and is animated, regenerative, and the immediate instrument and principal seat of the soul, inasmuch, moreover, as it seems to partake of the nature of another more divine body, and is transfused by divine animal heat, it obtains remarkable and most excellent powers, and is analogous to the essence of the stars.[37]

Nor should the fact be overlooked that Newton, too, was often thought to be resorting to a non-material force (gravity) in his explanation of heavenly motions. While it may be true that he was, in fact, content to describe and analyze phenomena mathematically without accounting for the causes of what he described, the *Principia* nonetheless produced a rash of accusations of mysticism from the Cartesians, who insisted that a force could not operate at a distance and that all explanations must include a description

[37] *Anatomical Exercises on The Generation of Animals; to which are added Essays on Parturition; On the Membranes, and Fluids of the Uterus; and on Conception* (1651), in *The Works of William Harvey*, ed. Robert Willis (London: The Sydenham Society, 1847), p. 510. For a discussion of Harvey's metaphysics and vitalism generally, see T. C. Allbut, *Science and Medieval Thought* (London: Clay, 1901).

of the strictly mechanical linkages at work.[38] The attribution to Newton of abandonment of Cartesian mechanics and embracing of the idea that force can operate at a distance was "the strongest obstacle to the acceptance of Newtonianism." Great scientists like Huygens and Leibniz attempted, but in vain, to restore vitality to the view that motion can take place only by matter pushing on matter.[39] The effect of this somewhat controversial idea of gravity on the relationship of science to theology, and hence on the matter of diagnosis, is well illustrated by John Locke's reaction to the issue:

I admit that I said (*Essay on Human Understanding,* Book II, ch. VIII, par. 11) that body acts by impulse and not otherwise. This also was my view when I wrote it and even now I cannot conceive its action in any other way. But since then I have been convinced by the judicious Mr. Newton's incomparable book that there is too much presumption in wishing to limit the power of God by our limited conceptions. The gravitation of matter toward matter in ways inconceivable to me is not only a demonstration that God, when it seems to Him good, can put into bodies powers and modes of acting which are beyond what can be derived from our idea of body or explained by what we know of matter; but it is furthermore an incontestable instance that He has really done so. I shall therefore take care to correct this passage in the new edition of my book.[40]

[38] See the excellent discussion of this aspect of Newton's work and resulting misconceptions of it in Hall, *The Scientific Revolution,* pp. 246–76, especially the quotation from a letter by Newton (pp. 273–74) that is an explicit denial of any resort to occult forces: "It is inconceivable that inanimate brute matter should, without the mediation of something else, which is not material, operate upon and affect other matter without mutual contact. . . . That gravity should be innate, inherent, and essential to matter, so that one body may act upon another at a distance through a vacuum, without the mediation of anything else, by and through which their action and force may be conveyed from one to another, is to me so great an absurdity that I believe no man who has in philosophical matters a competent faculty of thinking, can ever fall into it."

[39] See Alexandre Koyré, *Newtonian Studies* (Cambridge, Mass.: Harvard University Press, 1965), pp. 115–38.

[40] Quoted in *ibid.,* p. 155.

It must have appeared to many others, at it did to Locke, that, far from tending to exclude or limit the role of God, the new science often served to affirm and reiterate it. Assertions from Huygens, Leibniz, and others that only matter can influence matter came too late for anyone to revise or reject the concept of witchcraft.[41] This skeptical view, of course, came to prevail but only as science narrowed its focus so as to exclude spiritual factors, not because scientific findings forced its acceptance. A strictly mechanistic conception of the human body, one that could have constituted a source of scientific opposition to findings of *maleficium* in the trials, was known as early in the century as 1628, when Harvey demonstrated the circulation of the blood. In some limited areas—theories of respiration, for example—this view was in fact adopted and produced a wealth of new insight.[42] But mechanism as a substitute for religious vitalism had to await the eighteenth century, a time when even Cotton Mather could call for the expulsion of metaphysics from medicine and could suggest "by the Laws of Matter and Motion to find out the Cause and Cure of Disease."[43] Until then "inaccurate diagnosis and complete misunderstanding of the cause of the diseases and accidents of the victims," as Ewen puts it,[44] was not a fair description of the role of medical men in the witch prosecutions. For the most part they were passive in the matters of accusation and trial, and when they did affirm the presence of witchcraft, they were reflecting not

[41] Probably the most vigorous debate on the gravity question is in H. G. Alexander, *The Leibniz-Clarke Correspondence* (New York: Barnes and Noble, 1964).

[42] See Leonard G. Wilson, "The Transformation of Ancient Concepts of Respiration in the Seventeenth Century," *Isis*, 51 (1960):161, 172:

The entire structure of Galenic physiology had been dismantled and its debris removed. Following the discovery of the circulation of the blood by Harvey, it had been shown in succession: that the lung tissue is composed of membranes surrounding minute air spores (Malpighi), that the blood circulates through these membranes in capillary vessels (Malpighi), that the essential requirement in respiration is a constant supply of fresh air (Hooke), that the change in colour of the blood during its passage through the lungs is due to its contact with the air (Lowen), that some portion of the air is removed in respiration (Mazow) and that this is the same portion of the air as is consumed by fire (Mazow).

[43] Quoted in Beal, "Cotton Mather," p. 112.

[44] *Witch Hunting and Witch Trials*, p. 113.

only the traditions of their general culture but also the relevant attitudes of the giants of their own scientific community.

In addition, it should be pointed out that it is not at all clear that doctrines of mechanism could not be made to serve the processes of prosecution. In 1692, for example, we find Thomas Brattle discussing the procedure for determining guilt that involves the accused touching the victim. If relief of the victim's suffering is forthcoming, the guilt of the accused is indicated:

> The Salem Justices, at least some of them, do assert that the cure of the afflicted persons is a natural effect of this touch; and they are so well instructed in the Cartesian philosophy, and in the doctrine of *effluvia*, that they undertake to give a demonstration how this does cure the afflicted persons; and the account they give of it is this; that by this touch, the venomous and malignant particles, that were ejected from the eye, do by this means, return to the body whence they came, and, so leave the afflicted persons pure and whole.[45]

The judges in Salem, like several of the doctors at the bedside, found scientific theory a valuable and relevant tool.

---

[45] Letter of Thomas Brattle, Fellow of the Royal Society, quoted in Burr, *Narratives*, p. 171.

VII

SCIENCE AND THE IDENTIFICATION
OF WITCHES: FEMALE EXPERTS

✠

The witchcraft cases presented many issues in which law relied upon science to aid in the discovery of witches. Scientific support for the belief that witches could cause sickness and death still left unsolved the identity of the witch in any given case. To any system of law, the identity of the accused is a vital question; to the settlers of Massachusetts, whose highly developed conceptions of due process of law permeated their legal order, this matter was a most essential element of the proceedings.[1] The priority accorded this view of justice was well expressed in part of a 1692 essay which responded to the protest that, if the law contained too many safeguards, no one would be convicted: "This is a dangerous Principle, and contrary to the mind of God, who hath appointed that there shall be good and clear proof against the Criminal; else he is not Providentially delivered into the hands of Justice,

---

[1] Willingness to let guilty persons free of the full punishment of the law because of a defect in the legal system can be aptly illustrated in the area of adultery. In 1631 it was declared to be a capital offense (*Records of the Governor and Company of the Massachusetts Bay*, 1:92). Six years later three persons were convicted and under ordinary circumstances would have been promptly executed (*ibid.*, p. 202). But a question was raised as to whether the law had been adequately publicized, and the opinion of the elders was sought. Then, as Governor Winthrop relates the story, "it was thought safest, that these three persons should be whipped and banished; and the law was confirmed and published" (Journal, 1:262–63).

to be taken off from the earth. Nor hath God exempted this case of Witchcraft from the General Rule. Besides, reason tells us, that the more horrid the Crime is, the more Cautious we ought to be in making any guilty of it."[2]

There were, of course, a variety of ways by which the identity of the witch in question could be established. One way was to see whether the touch of the suspected witch on the victim produced a remission in the sufferer, a method described in Thomas Brattle's famous letter of 1692. The confession of the witch was another proof, although it is in this connection that the question of mental disorder arose, discussed in the next chapter. In the Salem trials it was obvious to many that the accused were confessing merely in order to escape punishment, since repentant witches were spared the gallows.[3] The use of confessions to convict witches also involves the question of torture, and there is some evidence that it was used illegally in Massachusetts.[4]

Perhaps the most controversial method of proving the guilt of the accused involved the use of what was called "spectral evi-

[2] The essay is entitled *Some Miscellany Observations on our Present Debates respecting Witchcrafts.* The authorship is in doubt but is traditionally assigned to the Reverend Samuel Willard of the Old South Church (see Perry Miller, *The New England Mind: From Colony to Province,* pp. 204–6). The quotation is taken from p. 205.

[3] This disposition of confessed witches greatly undermined, almost destroyed, the theological base on which the whole society rested (see *ibid.,* pp. 200–4, 207–8).

[4] Torture was authorized by law, but only in certain cases after conviction: "It is ordered, decreed, and by this Court declared; that no man shall be forced by torture to confesse any crime against himselfe or any other, unles it be in some Capital case, where he is first fully convicted by clear and sufficient evidence to be guilty. After which, if the Case be of that nature that it is very apparent there be other Conspirators or Confederates with him; then he may be tortured, yet not with such tortures as be barbarous and inhumane" (*The Laws and Liberties of Massachusetts,* p. 50).

One complaint about torture in the witchcraft cases appears in a letter from John Proctor to certain ministers concerning his son: "My son William Proctor, when he was examin'd, because he would not confess that he was Guilty, when he was Innocent, they tyed him Neck and Heels till the Blood gushed out of his Nose, and would have kept him so 24 Hours, if one more Merciful than the rest, had not taken pity on him, and caused him to be unbound. These actions are very like the Popish Cruelties." Robert Calif printed the letter in his *More Wonders of the Invisible World* (1700); it is reprinted in Burr, *Narratives,* p. 363; see also *ibid.,* p. 363, n. 2.

dence." This was based upon the common belief that demons could take the form of a person and, as his specter, either inflict harm on the body of another person or simply appear and converse on some evil subject. In such a case, at the trial the victim would testify that the accused came to him on a certain occasion and acted in a witchly way; the defense of the accused that he was miles away or knew nothing of the incident would be quite beside the point because at the time in question it was his specter, not his person, that bore witness to his being a witch. The question of whether the testimony of the victim to this effect was admissible and, if so, what weight it should be given was troublesome in the Salem trials. The issue that proved of major importance in the trials was that of whether an innocent person could be represented by a specter. Under the influence of Judge Stoughton, in 1692 the court at Salem ruled that this was not possible.[5]

There was still another means of identifying the witch, namely, by the signs of guilt that could be discovered in an expert search of the accused's body. Any modern law enforcement official would find his task greatly simplified if he could have suspected persons examined for the presence of certain physical signs that would generally be accepted as strong evidence of guilt. The witchcraft investigations enjoyed just such an advantage, and they exploited it fully. The search for the so-called Devil's marks was sanctioned by all authorities. Michael Dalton, whose *Country Justice* was a cornerstone of precedent, described the signs as

> some big or little Teat upon their body, and in some secret place, where he (the Devil) sucketh them. And besides their sucking, the Devil leaveth other marks upon their body, sometimes like a blew spot or red spot, like a flea-biting; sometimes the flesh sunk in and hollow, (all which for a time may be covered, yea taken

[5] For a collection and discussion of English cases in which spectral evidence was admitted, both before and after the Salem trials, see Kittredge, *Witchcraft in Old and New England*, pp. 363–65. Perry Miller places much of the responsibility for the devastating use of spectral evidence on leading members of the Puritan clergy, who, although they came out in support of the proposition that the innocent could be represented, refrained from making an effective protest (see *The New England Mind: From Colony to Province*, pp. 193–95, n. 2, 198–200).

away, but will come again to their old form.) And these the
Devils marks be insensible, and being pricked will not bleed, and
be often in their secretest parts, and therefore require diligent and
careful search.[6]

The employment of this investigative technique was not without its critics, however. Thomas Brattle, for example, included
among his objections to the Salem trials the reliance on these
witch's marks. Speaking of this process of proof, he says: "They
are searched by a Jury; and as to some of them, the Jury brought
in, that [on] such or such a place there was a preternatural
excrescence. And I wonder what person there is, whether man
or woman, of whom it cannot be said but that, in some part of
their body or other, there is a preternatural excrescence. The term
is a very general and inclusive term."[7] There is also the remarkable
Connecticut document protesting witchcraft prosecutions that re-
quests "that ye unusuall excresencies found upon their bodies
ought not to be allowed as evidence against them without ye
approbation of some able physitians."[8] One of the two signers of
this document was a physician "of great ability."[9]

The reply that was made to objections of this sort relied heavily
on the authority of the scientists and their ability to make an
accurate differential diagnosis. Thus Cotton Mather responded:
"I add, why should not witches marks be searched for? The prop-
erties, the qualities of those marks are described by divers weighty
writers. I never saw any of those marks, but it is doubtless not
impossible for a surgeon, when he sees them, to say what are
magical."[10] Perhaps one of the "divers, weighty writers" to whom

[6] P. 273.

[7] Letter of October 8, 1692, in Burr, *Narratives*, p. 175.

[8] Quoted in John M. Taylor, *The Witchcraft Delusion in Colonial Connecticut*
(New York: Grafton Press, 1908), p. 74.

[9] See *Genealogical and Family History of the State of Connecticut*, 1 (1911):45.

[10] Quoted in Rossell Hope Robbins, *The Encyclopedia of Witchcraft and
Demonology* (New York: Crown Publications, 1959), p. 136. See also the statement of a physician to Henry IV of France, which equates skepticism on this point
with professional incompetence: "Writers who say that it is difficult to distinguish
devil's marks from natural blemishes, from a carbuncle, or from impetigo clearly
show that they are not good doctors" (*ibid.*).

Mather was referring was Mathew Hopkins, the famous witch-finder in England. In his well-known book, *The Discovery of Witches*, Hopkins constructed a dialogue concerned with this problem which identified more accurately than had Mather or the Connecticut petitioners the scientific experts whose authority and skills were involved. Hopkins sets about answering a number of questions, among them "Quereie 5. Many poore people are condemned for having a Pap, or Teat about them, whereas many People (especially antient People) are, and have been a long time, troubled with naturall excrescencies as Hemerodes, Piles, Child-bearing, &c." To this question Hopkins replies that the existence of witch's marks is supported by "many ancient skilfull matrons and midwives present when the women are tryed," who attest that "such token cannot in their judgments proceed from any of the above mentioned Causes."[11]

That it was, in fact, "matrons and midwives" who did the searching of the female accused, rather than surgeons, is borne out by the cases reported in both Massachusetts and the other colonies. Mather was probably referring to what may have been a common practice of assigning the formal responsibility for certain examinations to a medically trained male, while the actual search was done by women. In New Hampshire, for example, a magistrate (who was also a physician) issued to a constable one of the earliest search warrants to be found, authorizing the search of a house for a "child or an embryo of which a woman was said to be delivered. A bit irregularly, but with an eye to decency and expertness . . . , the warrant was addressed to two midwives and three other women, as well as to the constable."[12] In Massachusetts the first signature that appears on the report of the search conducted on the accused witch, Rebecca Nurse, in 1692 was "J. Barton Chyrugen," although it is clear from the papers in the case that he took no active part.[13] The names of nine women follow

---

[11] Hopkins' text is in Montague Summers, *The Discovery of Witches. A Study of Master Mathew Hopkins Commonly Call'd Witch Finder Generall* (London: Cayne Press, 1928). The question and answer quoted appear on p. 52.

[12] Quoted in Page, *Judicial Beginnings in New Hampshire*, p. 105.

[13] Quoted in *The Historical Collections of the Topsfield Historical Society*, 13:53.

Barton's. They had been ordered by the sheriff to examine six accused women. Their report was as follows: "The first three, namely: Bishop, Nurse; Proctor by diligent search have discovered a preternatural excrescence of flesh between ye pudendum and Anus much like to tetts and not vsuall in women and much vnlike to ye other three that hath been search by us and that they were in all three women neer ye same place."[14] All six were executed as witches.[15] Below is the petition for a second examination that Rebecca Nurse submitted to the court in Salem. It is provided not only because it illustrates the point just made concerning the exclusive role of women experts regarding female accused but also because it presents dramatically the conflicts engendered by reliance on these experts and their knowledge.

The humble petission of Rebeccah Nurse of Salem Village.
Humbly Sheweth
That whereas sum women did search your Petissioner at Salem, and I did then conceive for sum Supernaturall Mark, and then one of the sd. women which is knoun to be, the Moaste Antiente skilfull, prudent person of them all as to any such conceive: Did express herself to be: of a Contrary opinion from the Rest, and Did then Declare that she saw nothing in or about yoer Honor's poare pettissioner But what might Arise from a Naturall cause: and I then rendered the said persons a sufficient knoun reason as to myself of the moueing cause thereof which was by Exceeding weaknesses: decending partly from an ouerture of Nature and difficult Exigences that hath Befallen me in the times of my travells And therefore your pettissioner: Humbly prayes that your Honour's would be pleased to admitt of some other women to Enquire into this Great: concern; those that are Moast Grand wise and skillfull; namely: Mrs.: Higgenson senr: Ms. Durkstone: Ms: Woodberry two of them being Midwives: Ms. Parter:

[14] Quoted in *ibid.*, pp. 52–53.
[15] According to Hutchinson, there is one additional case of an execution even when no witch's marks were found, that of Ann Hibbins in 1655 (*History of the Colony*, p. 187). Hutchinson notes also that the judges refused to accept the verdict of guilt brought in by the jury and the case was appealed to the General Court, "where the popular clamour prevailed against her and the miserable old woman was condemned and executed" (*ibid.*).

together with such others, as may be choasen on that Account: before I am Brought to my triall: All which I hoape your Honour's will Take into your prudent consideration; and find it requisite soe to doe: for my life lyes now in your Hands, under God: And Being Conscious of my owne Innocency. I humbly begg that I may have liberty to manifest it to the wourld partly by the Meanes abouesaid: And your Poare pettissioner shall Evermore pray as in duty bound Sc.

REBECCA NURSE:
hir Marke †[16]

Another examination was made a few hours later, not only of Nurse but of Bishop and Proctor as well. It was, however, done by the same persons as the first one. This time on the person of Rebecca Nurse the examiners found that "instead of that Excresence within mentioned it appears only as dry skin without sense . . . and that the piece of flish . . . formerly seen is gone and only dry skin nearer to ye anus in another place."[17] The jury refused to convict her, and it was only after it was forced to reconsider its position by the judges that it returned a verdict of guilty. Then Rebecca Nurse was hanged.[18]

These incidents reveal that expert testimony could change radically within a span of only a few hours, and that the searching women sometimes differed among themselves concerning what they observed. Nevertheless, from the outset, such evidence seems to have been considered important in the witchcraft cases. In the very first trial, that of Margaret Jones of Charlestown in 1648, Winthrop noted that "she had (upon search) an apparent teat in her secret parts as fresh as if it had been newly sucked, and after it had been scanned, upon a forced search that was withered, and another began on the opposite side."[19] This procedure was used early and widely. In the search of a Connecticut witch the women found "on her secret parts Just within ye lips of ye same growing within sid[,] sumewhat as broad[,] and reach without ye lips

---

[16] *The Historical Collections of the Topsfield Historical Society*, 13:55–56.
[17] *Ibid.*, pp. 56–57.
[18] Calif, *More Wonders of the Invisible World*, pp. 258–59.
[19] John Winthrop, Journal, 2:344.

of ye same about an Inch and half long lik in shape to a dogs eare[,] which wee apprehend to be unusuall to women."[20] In Virginia, it is reported, juries of women were impaneled in 1675 and 1679 to search " 'according to the 118th chapter of Dalton' for the Devil's marks."[21] As late as 1705 a Virginia jury of women reported the accused was "not like them nor noe Other woman that they knew of, having two things like tetts on her private parts of a Black Coller, being Blacker that the Rest of her Body."[22] In Maryland there was an unusual case of a woman who, after she had been called a witch by others, petitioned the court for what was, in effect, an injunction against the defamation. In the petition she asked for an examination by able women to show that she was in fact not a witch.[23]

There were cases, as has been indicated, in which the accused was executed as a witch in spite of the finding of searchers that she had no witch's marks. Their absence was no obvious sign of innocence, although there is some indication of a belief that a person could not be a witch if he had no physical signs. What may have been a common view in this matter was expressed by Thomas Cooper, who had been appointed to guard one Mary Parsons, accused of witchcraft. There seems to have been a question as to whether she or her husband had murdered their child. She told Cooper that she could prove her husband was the witch in question. To this, the guard replied, "Methinks, if he were a witch, there would be some apparent sign or mark of it upon his body, for they say witches have teats upon some part or other of their body; but so far as I hear there is not any such apparent thing upon his body."[24]

[20] Quoted in Taylor, *The Witchcraft Delusion in Colonial Connecticut*, p. 43.

[21] Burr, *Narratives*, p. 436.

[22] *Ibid.*, p. 442. In this same case, however, one group of women who were summoned to perform the search refused to do so (*ibid.*, p. 440).

[23] Francis N. Parke, *Witchcraft in Maryland* (Baltimore: n.p., 1937), pp. 44–47.

[24] Quoted in Poole, "Witchcraft in Boston," p. 140. The marks found on men were mostly of the kind that "being pricked will not bleed," as Dalton puts it. The phenomenon of supernumerary breasts (polymastia) may also have been involved. This condition is twice as frequent in men as in women (Max Thorek, *Plastic Surgery of the Breast and Abdominal Wall* [Springfield, Ill.: Charles C Thomas, 1942], pp. 94–101).

The witchcraft cases were not the only instances in which law administrators called upon the female experts. There are many instances, for example, where the possible offense of fornication was involved, in which the midwives were ordered to make a search to find if a woman was or had been pregnant.[25] Even in civil actions, where there was a question as to whether a female plaintiff in an assault and battery case had suffered injuries, or as to what kind they were, it was a female independent expert who made the search and reported to the court.[26] In some cases, although the sexual identity of the searching expert is not mentioned, the inference is quite strong that it was a midwife rather than any male, for example, "Robert Wyor & John Farland beeing indited for ravishing two yong girles, the fact confessed by the girles, & both upon search found to have bin defloured."[27] There is also, however, some evidence that law enforcement officials did not always consider themselves bound to refrain from engaging in searches on some occasions. There is the deposition of the Constable of Salisbury in the *Massachusetts Archives*, in the case of Eunice Cole. He said that "being about to strip Eunice Cole to be whipt . . . looking upon her breast under one of her breasts (I think her left breast) I saw a blue thing." He then asked that the court send some women to take a look for themselves.[28]

The female experts in the witchcraft cases, in seeking to distinguish the natural from the unnatural, to identify what was usual or unusual in women, were involved in somewhat the same difficulties as were encountered by the physicians faced with explaining difficult cases of death or disease. It was a specialized problem of differential diagnosis. In regard to the witch's marks, there was here also a residual category of "witchcraft" that piety demanded they respect. Their task was more limited, however, in

[25] See the cases in *Quarterly Court of Essex County*, 4:91 (1669); 5:291 (1674); 8:145 (1681); and in "Records of the Suffolk County Court 1671–1680," in *Publications of the Colonial Society of Massachusetts*, 29:91, 185. See also Semmes, *Crimes and Punishments in Early Maryland*, p. 192.

[26] *Quarterly Court of Essex County*, 2:443–46.

[27] *Records of the Court of Assistants*, 2:121.

[28] Massachusetts Archives, Massachusetts State Library, State House, Boston, Mass., Vol. 135, p. x3.

the sense that the whole of their judgment turned on familiarity with anatomy, particularly that of the female genitalia and, to some extent, with the field that is now known as gynecology. It was theoretically possible for them, as for the physicians, to declare that, although they had never seen a growth, a structure, or an organ that appeared as it did in a particular accused woman, still there was probably a natural explanation for it—one that, as yet, they had not encountered. Such a position would certainly have made convictions more difficult in some cases and might well have saved some lives.

The explanation of why this was not done must rest, in part, on their reluctance to reject witchcraft and thereby to appear to be atheists. But, as was true with the doctors, such a clinging to orthodoxy is only part of the picture. It should be realized, moreover, that such an affirmation would not have amounted to the wholesale rejection of traditional belief that would have been involved in a physician's declaration that sickness and death could not be, and in any given case was not, caused by the power of spirits. It would have been quite possible to believe wholeheartedly in spiritual interferences in human affairs, even to believe that a certain person was a witch and had produced the *maleficium* alleged, while at the same time believing that one part of the case against the individual was not proved. The judgment of the midwives, in other words, was a more circumscribed piece of expertise. The conflict of opinion in the case of Rebecca Nurse and the others indicates that a finding of "non-witch" could be made with little fear of betraying any sympathy with the forces of evil. Yet there must have been some reluctance of this sort involved.

In looking for an explanation, one must first appreciate the precarious position of the female medical practitioner and the midwife (the two were virtually the same during these times). Margaret Jones, hanged in Boston in 1648, is a case in point. She seems to have been a medical practitioner who encountered the censure of her male colleagues. Fiske describes her as having "had some sensible ideas about medicine. She disapproved of wholesale bleeding and violent emetics, and used to work cures by means of herb tonics and other simple prescriptions."[29] But the sufferings of some of those she treated seem to have continued, and their complaints might well have easily ripened into the accusation of witchcraft.

There was a tradition of associating female quackery with witchcraft that can be seen in the preamble to Henry VIII's statute regulating medical practice:

> For asmuch as the science and cunning of physick and surgery, is daily within this realm, exercised by a great multitude of ignorant persons, of whom the greater part have no manner of insight in the same, nor any other kind of learning, that common artificers as smiths, weavers and women, boldly and accustomably take upon them great cures and things of great difficulty in which they partly use sorcery and witchcraft; partly apply such medicines unto the disease as to be noxious and nothing meet therefore to the high displeasure of God great infamy to the faculties and the grievous hurt damage and destruction of many of the King's liege people most specially of them that cannot discern the uncunning from the cunning.[30]

Even disregarding the peculiar role of women in medical practice, the fact must also be considered that there was a strong relationship between diagnostic procedures and resort to occult knowledge. Astrology, for example, was a means of forecasting the course of an illness that roused the ire of the clergy for its implicit determinism; the esoteric nature of the pharmacopoeia presented another link with dark knowledge.[31] In short, medical judgment itself sometimes contained a mysterious element that made distinguishing between it and conjuration a difficult matter. All of these suspicious circumstances were apparently put together into a sinister pattern at least as early as 1441, when the Duchess of Gloucester was accused of witchcraft, an accusation which was, in

[29] John Fiske, *New France and New England* (Boston: Houghton Mifflin, 1902), p. 145.
[30] 3 Hen. 8, c. 11, 1511–12.
[31] Kocher, *Elizabethan England*, pp. 201–24.

part, "owing to her 'uncanny' knowledge of medicine and astrology."[32]

There was still another danger of impiety in seeking non-witchly interpretations of the searchers' observations. The Puritans would no doubt have seconded Nicholas Remy's argument that "to make nature the standard and measure of all things, to believe only what was credible, in effect tied the hands and circumscribed the power of God."[33] Some room had to be left for incredible and, more important, supernatural events.

In view of the colonial problem of controlling quackery and the risk of accusations of witchcraft taken by medical practitioners, it is quite understandable that the midwives might hesitate to question any part of orthodox belief and practice and tend to resolve all questionable cases against the accused. Something also needs to be said about the quality of the expertise that was exercised in the searches. Our assumption that physicians might have disavowed the notion of the spiritual causation of disease and death was partly based on the premise that the growth of knowledge in the medical field was accelerating and that they were generally aware of the exploding boundaries of scientific insight. In both these respects, the position of the midwife is quite dissimilar to that of the physician.

As to the substantive knowledge of the female sexual anatomy that was involved, it is difficult to assess exactly whether, considered in the abstract, it was sufficient to permit recognition of the "marks" as natural phenomena. While it is true that advances in female anatomy were made as the study of anatomy as a whole progressed, this field presented some real difficulties. For example, a widely used anatomical text by the Italian Mondino (1270[?]–1326) was based on the female anatomy of animals,[34] and the

[32] Lea, *Inquisition*, 3:467–68; and Copeman, *Doctors and Disease in Tudor Times*, p. 136. These problems were not peculiar to Massachusetts. See Walter R. Steiner, "A Contribution to the History of Medicine in the Province of Maryland, 1636–1671," *Bulletin of the Johns Hopkins Hospital*, 13 (1902):194.

[33] Quoted in John L. Teall, "Witchcraft and Calvinism in England," *Journal of the History of Ideas*, 23 (1962):35.

[34] Arturo Castiglioni, *A History of Medicine* (New York: Alfred A. Knopf, 1941), p. 344.

most popular basic source book for midwives, Roslin's *Rosengarten* (imitated in English by Thomas Raynalde in 1540 under the title *The Byrthe of Mankynde*), appeared in 1513, before the corrections stimulated by Vesalius had been made.[35] Raynalde's version was still being issued, largely unchanged, as late as 1676.[36] Vesalius himself provided no assistance on this score. His textual descriptions of female sex organs are sketchy, and the drawings that appeared in the *Fabrica* are counted as among the most inaccurate in an otherwise outstanding set of illustrations.[37] But it would be quite wrong to say that this field was neglected entirely. As early as the middle of the fifteenth century Ferrari had described the female ovary,[38] and work on the internal organs by

[35] For a description of an earlier but unprinted treatise, see J. H. Aveling, "Account of the Earliest English Work on Midwifery and the Diseases of Women," *Obstetrical Journal of Great Britain and Ireland*, 2 (1875):73. The 1545 and subsequent editions of *The Byrthe of Mankynde* included several anatomical plates from Vesalius' *Fabrica* (see J. W. Ballantyne, *The "Byrthe of Mankynde": Its Author, Editions and Contents* [London: Sherratt and Hughes, 1909], pp. 343–48); see also L. Clendening, *Source Book of Medical History* [New York: Hoeber, 1942], pp. 170–79).

[36] There were fourteen editions altogether (see Ballantyne, *The "Byrthe of Mankynde,"* pp. 324–25).

[37] J. B. de C. M. Saunders and Charles D. O'Malley, eds., in the *Illustrations from the Works of Andreas Vesalius* (New York: World, 1950), p. 170, comment:

This extraordinary figure of the female genitalia has been the subject of much comment. Some have called it "monstrous" and others have implied that a Freudian quirk in the author had resulted in its assuming a resemblance to the male organ. However, if one is familiar with the circumstances under which Vesalius obtained the specimen, it is not difficult to interpret. It was obtained from the body of a woman who had been the mistress of a certain monk. Vesalius and his pupils, hearing of her death, snatched the body from the tomb, but, unfortunately, the monk together with the parents of the girl complained of the outrage to the city magistrates so that the anatomist and his students were compelled to dismember and free the body from all skin as rapidly as possible to prevent its being recognized. Since they had stolen the body expressly to examine the female organs, the best they could do was to encircle the external genitalia with a knife, split the symphysis and excise the vagina and uterus in one piece after severance of the urethra. Later, the uterine cavity was exposed by sectioning the body longitudinally and turning up the anterior half. We imagine that the uterine tubes were lost in the hurried method of preparation.

A somewhat different story is told in Henry Morley, "Andreas Vesalius," in *Toward Modern Science*, ed. Robert M. Palter (New York: Noonday Press, 1961), 2:76–77.

[38] Castiglioni, *A History of Medicine*, p. 368.

leading anatomists such as Fallopius (1523–1562)[39] and Graaf (1641–1673) continued.[40] Truly outstanding figures in medical history also participated in the research, including Ambroise Paré, the great surgeon (1510[?]–1590), who conducted a small school for midwives in Paris,[41] and John Weyer, who not only pioneered in psychological medicine but also invented a speculum for examination of the vagina and described retention of menstrual flow and occlusion of the neck of the uterus.[42]

The concern of the searching midwives, however, was with pathology of the external organs, and historical judgment is rendered most difficult here. Around the turn of the seventeenth century some descriptions of the external organs were made, for example, by Adriaan van den Spieghel (1578–1625),[43] and Fallopius had included mention of the clitoris in his work.[44] Moreover, in 1579 there had been a fairly complete enumeration of the relevant anatomy by Cabial, surgeon to the King of France.[45] There was also a treatise (1595) on gynecological rarities by Van Granfenberg (1530–1598).[46] Whether these and other contributions[47] brought the things observed by the searching women into the realm of what was understood as natural is impossible to know. All we can say is that the probability of seeing a natural phenomenon rather than a witch's mark would have been increased if extant knowledge had been applied to the searching process. We know, for example, that when a really first-rate medical mind participated in a search for witches' marks the result was exculpatory. During the prosecution of the Lancashire witches in 1634 to 1635 four suspected women were ordered searched by ten midwives,

[39] Nordenskiold, *The History of Biology*, p. 104.

[40] *Ibid.*, pp. 171–73.

[41] Kate C. H. Mead, *A History of Women in Medicine* (Haddam, Conn.: Haddam, 1938), p. 393.

[42] Zilboorg, *A History of Medical Psychology*, p. 208.

[43] James V. Ricci, *The Genealogy of Gynaecology* (New York: Blakeston, 1943), p. 343.

[44] André Pecker, *Hygiène et maladies de la femme au cours des siècles* (Paris: Decasta, 1961), p. 17.

[45] *Ibid.*

[46] Ricci, *The Genealogy of Gynaecology*, p. 327.

[47] See *ibid.*, pp. 285–333.

six surgeons, and no less a figure than William Harvey, then physician to Charles I. Of the four women examined by this panel, three were cleared completely. On the fourth it was reported there were "two things which may be called teats." But these were not accepted as incriminating evidence: "The first in shape like a teat of a bitch but in our judgement nothing but the skin as it will be drawn out after the application of leeches. The second is like the nipple or teat of a woman's breast but of the same colour with the rest of the skin, without any hollowness or issue of any blood or juice to come from thence."[48]

There were a host of reasons why nothing resembling the judgment of a William Harvey was applied to the Massachusetts cases. An understanding of the role of the midwives may be advanced by reference to the gap that generally existed between new knowledge in medicine and its acceptance and implementation in common practice. In the case of female practitioners, the gap was further widened by virtue of their exclusion from any formal medical education in the English universities,[49] by their lack of any significant amount of non-medical education (only one of the eight examining women in Rebecca Nurse's case could write her own name; the others each made "hir Marke"), and by their general non-participation in the intellectual life of the community at large.[50] They thus tended to be insulated from printed works and from any feeling for the dynamic growth of knowledge during the period of the great scientific advances. It is not at all surprising that there is not the smallest sign that any of the women whom the law called upon hesitated to assign to the realm of witch-

[48] The report is quoted from Keele, *William Harvey*, p. 71. For discussion of the probability of Harvey's disbelief in witches, see Notestein, *A History of Witchcraft in England*, pp. 160–63.

[49] Some English women were educated at Italian medical schools, however (see Mead, *A History of Women in Medicine*, p. 401).

[50] This is well illustrated by an entry in John Winthrop's Journal concerning a Mrs. Hopkins "who was fallen into a sad infirmity, the loss of her understanding and reason which had been growing upon her diverse years, by occasion of her giving herself wholly to reading and writing, and had written many books. . . . For if she had attended her household affairs, and such things as belong to women, and not gone out of her way and calling to meddle in such things as are proper for men, whose minds are stronger, etc., she had kept her wits" (2:225).

craft things they observed which were beyond their experience. It may be suggested further that this commitment to a wholly static state of knowledge was supported by the unhospitable attitude of a male-dominated medical profession, which was not likely to react favorably to attitudes that seemed contrary to its own. It is true that direct professional competition between men and women in the area of obstetrics and gynecology was yet to come. It was only during the course of the seventeenth century that these matters began to enter the list of subjects taught men in their medical preparation,[51] and formal lectures on obstetrics did not take place in America until they were instituted by the famous Dr. William Shippen, Jr., in 1765.[52] Nonetheless, it would be a mistake to explain the role of the midwife in the trials strictly on the basis of a lack of any direct male participation in her particular medical activity during the times in question, since there was a fair amount of "general practice" by women, which did put them directly in contact with men. The male attitude was probably more a function of their reaction to women in medicine generally than of any question as to where the formal lines of professional competence fell between the two sexes. At any rate, the women tended to keep "in line" and were among the last members of the seventeenth-century medical community to voice any opinions that were new to their profession.

[51] Castiglioni, *A History of Medicine*, p. 569.
[52] Packard, *History of Medicine in the United States*, 1:53. See also Herbert Thomas, *Chapters in American Obstetrics* (Springfield, Ill.: Charles C Thomas, 1932).

VIII

THE DEFENSE OF INSANITY

✠

One of the most widely held views concerning the witchcraft trials is that virtually all of the persons who were prosecuted as witches were mentally ill. Regardless of how accurate this belief may be in so far as the Continental cases are concerned, it cannot be applied to the Massachusetts experience merely because of a presumed analogy to the European trials.

The first factor supporting the distinction between the two is the firm establishment of the defense of insanity in the common law of England before the American colonization was undertaken.[1] This defense would operate to prevent mentally ill persons from being convicted of *any* offense. Mental illness is, of course, a concept that has to be considered in its historical context. In Massachusetts, for example, a specific statute that was enacted in 1641 was phrased to reflect the two major considerations that were relevant to all the Puritan experience, religion and reason, made it clear that mental abnormality, along with other extenuating conditions, was not to be passed over in assessing criminal liability in the Bay Colony. It read: "Children, Idiots, Distracted persons, and

---

[1] See Sheldon Glueck, *Mental Disorder and the Criminal Law* (Boston: Little, Brown, 1925), p. 125. The defense also seems to have been known to the heresy prosecutions, at least in the early stages of the Inquisition. See the case of the heretic Eon de l'Etoile, whose insanity saved him from punishment, described in Lea, *Inquisition*, 1:66.

all that are strangers or new comers to our plantation, shall have such allowances and dispensations in any Case whether Criminal or other as religion and reason require."[2]

There is, furthermore, ample evidence that this statute was no mere pious reference, to be ignored in practice. Its application can be seen in several instances. In one case a stranger to the Colony, accused of stealing silver from a box that was found floating in the harbor, was acquitted on the grounds that "it was not usuall" to give up anything so found in his country.[3] Nor was the policy of dispensation for strangers limited to minor offenses of this sort. In one case that must have kindled many emotions, the kind of unfamiliarity that was implied in the term "stranger" stands out. An Indian who had committed forcible rape upon an English girl was held not liable for the usual death penalty. The trial court noted that "although in an ordinary consideration hee deserued death, yett considering hee was but an Indian, and therefore in an incapasity to know the horiblenes of the wickednes of this abominable act, with other cercomstances considered, hee was centanced by the Court to be seurly Whipt att the post and sent out of the country."[4] This was certainly a broad reading of the spirit of the law.

The insanity defense of the 1641 statute was also part of the active jurisprudence of the Colony. There was, for example, the fornication prosecution in which the accused woman was discharged, "the court judging by her carriages and testimonies concerning her that shee was a distempered crazy woman."[5] So too with a Mrs. Wilson, who was charged with frequently absenting herself from the public ordinances. She was dismissed from the court after it had been informed that she was "distempered in her head."[6]

In seeking to determine the role of the defense of insanity in the witchcraft cases, however, very few things can be said with certainty. There is only one instance in which a person charged

2 The Body of Liberties, No. 52 in *The Colonial Laws of Massachusetts*, p. 45.
3 *Publications of the Colonial Society of Massachusetts*, 30:1156.
4 *Records of Plymouth*, 6:98.
5 *Publications of the Colonial Society of Massachusetts*, 29:436.
6 *Quarterly Court of Essex County*, 4:88.

with witchcraft seems to have been discharged or acquitted on this ground, that of Elizabeth Johnson of Andover, granddaughter of Reverend Dane of that village. She was convicted in 1692 but was reprieved because she was "simplish." Her grandfather described Elizabeth, who had confessed to being a witch, as "but simplish at best."[7]

As to those who were executed as witches, the question of whether the defense might have been useful to them had it been in some way presented in their behalf involves more than the usual difficulties of such historically precarious speculation. The unfortunate fact is that we have no record at all of executions before 1692 on which to make a judgment. There are only a few fragmentary data. Regarding Margaret Jones, Governor Winthrop remarks that at her trial she "was very intemperate, lying notoriously, and railing upon the jury and witnesses, etc., and in the like distemper she died."[8] This description seems to show little more than extreme anger, which, under the circumstances, seems quite appropriate and not the behavior of a deranged person. There is nothing in the case of Ann Hibbins to suggest mental abnormality save the statement of a later writer that she was not "well settled in her mind."[9] As to Mrs. Lake and Mrs. Kendal, there is virtually no information at all except Reverend Hale's statement that both denied their guilt to the end.[10]

This leaves the fifth remaining pre-Salem execution which we know of, that of Mary Glover, to be accounted for. Here the material is more than fragmentary. In 1688 she was charged with using witchcraft on the children of John Goodwin so that they suffered greatly from fits. Cotton Mather provides us with the narrative. She confessed in open court to these deeds of witchcraft. "However," Mather continues,

> to make all clear, The Court appointed five or six Physicians one evening to examine her very strictly, whether she were not craz'd

[7] Quoted in Claude Moore Fuess, "Witches at Andover," *Proceedings of the Massachusetts Historical Society*, 70 (1953):14.

[8] Journal, 2:344.

[9] Poole, "Witchcraft in Boston," p. 139.

[10] *A Modest Inquiry*, pp. 408–9.

in her Intellectuals, and had not procured to herself by Folly and Madness the Reputation of a Witch. Diverse hours did they spend with her; and in all that while no Discourse came from her, but what was pertinent and agreeable; particularly when they asked her, What she thought would become of her soul? she reply'd "You ask me a very solemn Question, and I cannot well tell what to say to it." She own'd herself a Roman Catholick; and could recite her Pater Noster in Latin very readily; but there was one Clause or two alwaies too hard for her, whereof she said, "She could not repeat it, if she might have all the world." In the upshot, the Doctors returned her Compos Mentis; and Sentence of Death was pass'd upon her.[11]

In some respects Mrs. Glover was examined even more thoroughly than are criminal defendants today. The gathering for consultation of five or six doctors and their examination for "divers" hours compares quite favorably with the personnel and time now generally expended on the investigation of the criminal capacity of an accused person. But what is important here is the question of how well Mrs. Glover fared in the context of seventeenth-century Massachusetts law and psychology. This discussion should shed some light on the intriguing matter of why the insanity defense was not raised more often in the witchcraft cases.

The important thing to note in the Glover case is that it was in order to assess the state of her "Intellectuals" that the court called in the physicians. They, in turn, found her reasoning ability to be functioning well and, therefore, could claim for her no exemption from the processes of the criminal law. Her replies were "pertinent and agreeable," and her response to the specific question concerning her soul was completely consistent with an intact cognitive functioning. The focus of the examination was on her reason, a concern that appears in other criminal cases as well. In one instance a witness testified to an incident in which he was eating at the same table with the defendant, "and he did eat after all other had done and also licked the crumbs left on another's

---

[11] *Memorable Providences*, pp. 104–5.

plate—20 persons looking on at this and his other foolish tricks; I never could perceive he was at all ashamed, all of which makes it clear to me he hath not the use of his reason as other men."[12]

It is not at all surprising that reason here appears as the central and governing mental faculty. The preoccupation in Massachusetts with reasoning powers seems to illustrate what Gregory Zilboorg has called "the old tendency to consider all mental diseases as diseases of intellect or reason."[13] Of great importance was the fact that much of the then most recent work in human biology served to confirm and support a conception of insanity that was rooted in the malfunctioning of the intellect. Viewing modern "psychiatry proper" as being concerned primarily with emotional disorders, Zilboorg suggests that, looking back in time,

one may safely conclude that the trend toward the purely scientific which had developed in the medical world of the seventeenth century had comparatively little effect in the domain of psychiatry proper. Idiocy, cretinism, apoplexy, certain aspects of epilepsy, certain consequences of obvious brain injuries, and certain paralyses —a number of conditions which were due to actual brain defects, congenital or acquired—attracted the attention of the medical man. Passing over some of his flights of theoretical imagination, we should credit him with the successful advancement of our knowledge of what we learned in later centuries to recognize as organic diseases or defects of the central nervous system, which are accompanied with more or less gross mental disturbances—disturbances characterized mostly by deviations from normal intellectual functioning. . . . These allegedly purely intellectual disturbances were viewed as results of anatomical or physiological abnormalities. Even those diseases in which the symptoms were primarily emotional such as melancholy (known later as depression) and mania were viewed as conditions produced by organic causes. . . . The severe psychological conditions such as hysterical, convulsive states, or hyster-epilepsies as they were later called for a short period, the

[12] Testimony of John Trumble in the case of John Jackson, *Quarterly Court of Essex County*, 6:27.

[13] *A History of Medical Psychology*, p. 268; see also I. E. Drapkin, "Remarks on Ancient Psychopathology," *Isis*, 46 (1956):223.

ecstacies, the hallucinatory, persecutory states—in short, the vast majority of severe neuroses, so-called borderline conditions, and psychoses—were disregarded by those who felt themselves fully wedded to physics, chemistry and physiology.[14]

The colonists provided much evidence that they too were "fully wedded" to the physical sciences in their conception of mental illness. Cotton Mather discussed the physical basis of insanity in terms strikingly similar to the twentieth-century thesis of the biochemists and physiologists: "A great Philosopher observes and affirms, that the Clearness of our Fancy depends on the regular Structure of the Brain; by which it is fitted for the receiving and compounding of all Impressions with the more Regularity. In Fools the Brain is deformed. The Deformity is not easily noted in other people: But, no doubt, a smaller Difference than can be imagined may alter the Symmetry of the Brain, and so the Perspicuity of the Fancy."[15]

The therapy that was provided for mentally disordered persons was rational in that it followed this organic orientation of the etiology of their disease. On board the *Hannah & Elizabeth* on his way from Dartmouth to New England Dr. John Barton treated a Mrs. Killegroue for the "Maladie of Histericall vapors" with what was then fairly standard therapy, "suppository, a compound Clyster with Hisyricall Carmanitiue seeds and a stomachicall Emplaister."[16] Joane Brownstist's hysterical fits Barton treated with "Spiritt of Castar & oile of Amber seurall times."[17] In Salem Dr. Zerobabel Endicott's prescription for a distracted woman provides another example of the application of the pharmacopoeia to the problems of mental illness: "Tak milk of a Nurce that giues suck to a male child & also take a hee Cat & Cut of one

---

[14] *A History of Medical Psychology*, pp. 268–69. See also the discussion of the central role of reason in the conception of insanity in George Rosen, "Social Attitudes to Irrationality and Madness in Seventeenth and Eighteenth Century Europe," *Journal of the History of Medicine*, 18 (1936):220.

[15] *The Christian Philosopher*, pp. 234–35. A modern example is given in Sanford J. Fox, "Delinquency and Biology," *Miami Law Review*, 16 (1961):85–88.

[16] Quoted in Gordon, *Aesculapius Comes to the Colonies*, p. 6.

[17] *Ibid.*, p. 7.

of his ears or a piece of it & Lett it blede into the milk & then Lett the sick woman Drink it. Doe this three Times."[18]

Of course, this resort to drug therapy to put the humors back in balance often went hand in hand with prayer therapy. The amalgam is well illustrated by a letter of William Pynchon to Edward Hopkins in 1664, in which Pynchon declares, "Yet I must tell you that that hot subtell vapor which hath taken possession of her brain is hard to be removed though it may be much helped through Gods blessing uppon the event." He went on to recommend sweet milk and saffron so that "her body will be brought to a sweating temper which I conceive will be a good help to nature."[19]

It thus appears quite clear that intellectual functioning and the right use of reason were firmly established cornerstones of seventeenth-century conceptions of insanity both in and out of New England,[20] and it would be surprising indeed if a non-organic or functional view of mental illness—one that emphasized emotional pathology—had achieved any foothold at all in Puritan thinking. It must be recalled that "mind" was equated with "soul" and that nothing could be admitted as true that implied the possibility of sickness and, therefore, mortality, of the soul. The brain itself could become afflicted; a soul (and a mind) could be wicked, but not sick. Two hundred years later this same view was expressed by Pliny Earle, M.D., one of the leading American psychiatrists of the time:

> Were the arguments for the hypothesis that in insanity the mind itself is diseased tenfold more numerous than they are, and more weighty, I could not accept them. My ideas of the human mind are such that I cannot hold for a moment that it can be diseased, as we understand disease. That implies death as its final consequency, but Mind is eternal. In its organization, it was created for

18 Quoted in Dow, *Every Day Life in the Massachusetts Bay Colony*, pp. 183–84.
19 Quoted in *Proceedings of the Massachusetts Historical Society*, 48 (1914):56.
20 Insanity included, of course, the concept of lunacy. See, for example, testimony in 1676 concerning a man "outrageously mad and distracted" but only during "one parte of the moone" (*Quarterly Court of Essex County*, 6:228–29).

immortality, consequently, it is superior to the bodily structure, and beyond the scope of the wear and tear and disorganization and final destruction of the mortal part of our being.[21]

Seen in the context of the deeply religious position of the Massachusetts leadership, this mind-soul equation greatly reinforced the view that insanity was an entirely organic problem. This in turn, as Zilboorg has pointed out, perpetuated that notion that defects of reason are the essence of the symptomatology. Thus Mrs. Glover and several others were tested in their "Intellectuals."

Although only a heretic could openly suggest that the mind-soul could become defective, in its entirety or in its parts, yet it must have been clear to all that forms of insanity did exist and that there were unfortunate fellow humans whose reason was grossly impaired and whose behavior was grossly deranged. The reaction of the colonists to such people sheds some light on the problem at hand. If they harbored a harsh and punitive attitude towards those whom they recognized as being mentally ill, this might help to explain why mental illness was so infrequently used as a legal defense in the witchcraft cases. In other words, the consequence of ignoring a perceived mental illness would be imposition of the death penalty, and such a result would be acceptable if it were felt that the mentally ill ought to be punished anyway.

This thesis does not seem to be supportable, however, in spite of the general belief today that cruelty and abuse were the characteristic response to mental illness in colonial Massachusetts.[22] In the first place, the colonists shared with their English brethren what was for the times the quite progressive idea that care of the mentally ill was a public responsibility. In 1676 it was enacted that

> whereas there are distracted persons in some tounes, that are vnruly, whereby not only the families wherein they are, but others suffer much damage by them, it is ordered by this Court and the

[21] Quoted in Norman Dain, *Concepts of Insanity in the United States 1789–1865* (New Brunswick, N.J.: Rutgers University Press, 1964), pp. 64–65.

[22] See, for example, Albert Deutsch, *The Mentally Ill in America* (New York: Columbia University Press, 1949), pp. 25–39.

authoritie thereof, that the selectmen in all tounes where such persons are are hereby impowred & injoyned to take care of all such persons, that they doe not dmnify others; and also to take care & order the management of their estates in the times of their distemperature, so as may be for the good of themselues & families depending on them, and the charge to be paid out of the estates of all such persons where it may be had, otheruise at the publick charge of the toune such persons belong unto.[23]

Where insane persons were cared for at home, public funds bore the expense. There were, for example, orders for the payments of five pounds per year to parents for care of a distracted child[24] and of fifty shillings per year for care of a "distempered" child.[25] Even before the 1676 statute mentioned above, public guardians were imposed to look after the welfare of persons unable to care for themselves, as in the case of a Widow Willix; being in no capacity to "order and improve her estate by reason of a strange kind of distracted and distempered condition" from which she had been suffering for a long time, three men were appointed to take care of her estate, her comfortable subsistence, and to see that the building of her house was finished according to a contract entered into by her.[26]

This is not to say that the colonial attitude towards the mentally ill was always one of enlightened benevolence. In some instances, the particularly outrageous behavior of disturbed persons met with whipping and fines, as with two women who went naked to church in 1663.[27] Here, however, the inference that the women may be mentally disturbed may not have been shared by the colonists. There is also probably a good deal of truth to observations that the lot of the insane was not a happy one. "The insane poor languished in jails and almshouses, wandered aimlessly around the countryside, or were auctioned off to work for those who

[23] *Records of the Governor and Company of the Massachusetts Bay,* 5:80–81.
[24] *Ibid.,* 3:232.
[25] *Ibid.,* p. 363.
[26] *Quarterly Court of Essex County,* 3:149. See also the similar case of Widow Jackson in *ibid.,* p. 176.
[27] *Ibid.,* p. 64.

would support them at a minimal cost to the country. The well-to-do and middle class patients wasted away at home, chained in unheated attics, ill-fed and ill-clothed, and occasionally attended by doctors whose remedies included bleeding, purging and emetics."[28]

Even so, this picture does not seem to be one of a cruelty to the mentally ill approaching the intentional, into which can be fitted the explanation posited above—that the defense of insanity was not used in witchcraft cases because insanity was felt to be punishable. What may be enlightening, however, is the question of the absence of the defense from capital cases generally. It is a curious fact that even apart from the witchcraft cases there is not one criminal case involving the death penalty in which the defense of insanity is even alluded to. Of course, this omission may reflect the obvious and uniform sanity of capital offenders in Massachusetts. Yet there is at least one case where the assumed uniformity fails, that of Dorothy Talbie. She was convicted of murdering her daughter, Difficult Talbie, on December 4, 1638,[29] and was hanged two days later. Winthrop's account of this case includes a strong hint that the child's name derived from a serious illness of some sort. But what is more important is that his journal entry amounts to a virtual acknowledgment that Dorothy was mentally ill:

Dorothy Talbye was hanged at Boston for murdering her own daughter, a child of three years old. She had been a member of the church of Salem, and of good esteem for godliness, etc.; but, falling at difference with her husband, through melancholy or spiritual delusions, she sometimes attempted to kill him, and her children, and herself, by refusing meat, saying it was so revealed to her, etc. After much patience, and divers admonitions not prevailing, the church cast her out. Whereupon she grew worse; so as the magistrate caused her to be whipped. Whereupon she was reformed for a time, and carried herself more dutifully to her

[28] Norman Dain and Richard Carlson, "Social Class and Psychological Medicine," *Bulletin of the History of Medicine*, 33 (1959):445.
[29] *Records of the Governor and Company of the Massachusetts Bay*, 1:246.

husband, etc.; but soon after she was so possessed with Satan, that he persuaded her (by his delusions, which she listened to as revelations from God) to break the neck of her own child, that she might free it from future misery. This she confessed upon her apprehension; yet, at her arraignment, she stood mute a good space, till the governor told her she should be pressed to death, and then she confessed the indictment. When she was to receive judgment, she would not uncover her face, nor stand up, but as she was forced, nor give any testimony of her repentance, either then or at her execution. The cloth, which should have covered her face, she plucked off and put between the rope and her neck. She desired to have been beheaded, giving this reason, that it was less painful and less shameful. After a swing or two, she catched at the ladder.[30]

Perhaps a similar case is that of Mary Parsons, who was acquitted of witchcraft but was convicted of murdering her child in 1651.[31] Of her, Samuel Drake remarks that she was permanently insane.[32] Probably one reason for the absence of the insanity defense is the fact that there was no defense counsel involved in these cases. Without some such assistance an accused person would perhaps not plead insanity on his own. Yet the Glover case is one instance where the judges looked into this matter entirely on their own, so it must be acknowledged that there was at least some means by which the question could be raised in the prosecution process without the intervention of partisan lawyers.

Another possible explanation for the absence of the defense is the very limited use the colonists made of capital punishment. Of the seven common-law felonies for which death was the penalty under English law—homicide, rape, burglary, arson, robbery, larceny, and mayhem—the Massachusetts law recognized only the first two.[33] There was no vague category of "felony," as there was in England, for which the death penalty would be inflicted. Whenever the word "felony" was used in Massachusetts,

---

[30] Journal, pp. 282–83.
[31] Records of the Governor and Company of the Massachusetts Bay, 3:229.
[32] Drake, The Witchcraft Delusion in New England, p. 66.
[33] The Laws and Liberties of Massachusetts, p. 6.

it seems to have been an imprecise term meaning nothing more than "serious."[34] Restriction in the use of the death penalty can also be seen in statutes, unknown in English law, that authorized it only upon the third commission of the same offense.[35] And, of course, the numerous English capital crimes of purely statutory origin, such as "congregations and confederacies holden by Masons,"[36] were completely absent from Massachusetts law. One cannot but conclude that one of the major innovations of Massachusetts lawmaking was a greatly reduced use of capital punishment.[37]

It may not be amiss to speculate that concomitant with this limited definition of capital crimes was the attitude that, when an offense that had been denounced as capital was committed, the full rigor of the law should be felt. Account had been taken of the necessity for allowing for human failings, such as provisions for reformation of offenders, in the definition of what was capital and what was not, and the process largely resulted in a narrowing of the former category. After this legislative decision there was very little room left for considering the individual circumstances of the murderer or the witch, even when they were as striking as were the delusions of Dorothy Talbie. While there is no evidence that this view was verbalized, the assumption that it did prevail may make more intelligible the approach the colonists took to capital offenders generally.

Regarding witchcraft specifically, however, we must keep in mind that, whatever tendency there was for the courts to be alert for signs of insanity, its recognition depended upon the use or misuse of intellect and reason by those accused. It thus becomes highly important to observe that there was nothing irrational,

---

[34] For example, in 1671 Alice Thomas was convicted of "felonious theft" but was sentenced only to make treble restitution and to public humiliation (*Publications of the Colonial Society of Massachusetts*, 29:82–83).

[35] "Burglary and Robbery," in *The Laws and Liberties of Massachusetts*, pp. 4–5.

[36] Dalton, *Country Justice*, p. 276.

[37] I am grateful to Mr. Geoffry Paul Hellman for making available to me his 1965 Honors Thesis from Harvard College, in which he thoughtfully develops and documents this matter of restricting the death penalty.

nothing evincing defective reason, in the practice of witchcraft *per se.* We may tend today to think that anyone who seriously confesses to the perpetration of such deeds needs to have his head examined, but in the view of the seventeenth century he needed only to be punished, for the same reasons that a murderer was punished. A witch's confession and the testimony of victims and witnesses were all entirely reasonable to the uncraz'd intellectuals of the society. Virtually everyone fully believed that such things as were described could easily take place. Not only was witchcraft consistent with the functioning of normal intelligence and reason, it was, in a very significant sense, anticipated, awaited, and almost welcomed by the keenest minds of Puritan Massachusetts. It was seen as rational within a broad social context, rather than involving only the mental ability of individuals.

Appreciation of this last point depends upon knowledge of the particular form and nature of the Puritan religious beliefs on which the Colony was founded and the course of their evolution during most of the seventeenth century. Perry Miller has traced these beliefs in a brilliant study to which no summarizing can do full justice, but at the heart of the matter was the doctrine of the contract or federal covenant which the Puritan community had with God. Appreciation of this covenantal relationship is central to approaching any aspect of the history of colonial Massachusetts, and it is of major importance in understanding why insanity was barely mentioned in the witchcraft experience, especially in the events of 1692 and 1693. The covenant related to society as a single entity and was quite distinct from the individual's relations with his deity. It had, according to Miller, three distinct features:

> It has to do with conduct here and now, with visible success or tangible failure. Secondly, since a society cannot be rewarded in heaven for its obedience . . . and cannot be punished in hell . . . it must perforce contract with the Almighty for external ends. Its obedience, in short, means prosperity, its disobedience means war, epidemic or ruin. . . . In the third place, a community is not joined to God by so irrevocable a contract as will endure no matter how depraved it becomes. . . . If a society, no matter how many

103

saints may still be in it, sinks so deep into corruption that its abominations call for destruction, then the national covenant is ended.[38]

In such a view, the adversities suffered in New England could not be accidents or merely the logical concomitants of wilderness living. They were the consequences of breaches of the covenant, "exquisitely proportioned to the amount of depravity" in the community. Spiritual impurity bred hardship. Repentance, fasting, days of humiliation, etc., purged the sin and restored prosperity and peace. In the context of this ideological structure, the hanging of Margaret Jones in 1648 can be seen as the Puritan's performance of the secular side of the covenant—the suppression of vice. This cleaving to the path of godliness through law enforcement by a society enjoying a special relationship to its God presumably was as efficacious in keeping the community "covenanted" as was other related activity, such as keeping the community free from heretical opinion or maintaining proper intercongregational relationships. It was, in short, one aspect of a true society of God and a part of the example New England was setting for the rest of the world. Certainly there was no laxity in the judicial part of the demonstration, for, as Governor Bradford of Plymouth Plantation observed, "the churches look narrowly to their members and the magistrates over all, more strictly than in other places."[39]

In addition, there was another possible significance to criminal acts, including witchcraft. On the one hand, the sure administration of the criminal law was, as has been suggested, a covenantal obligation and was part of the light that was to shine "round the world from the city on a hill." On the other hand, the social harm produced by criminal conduct might have been felt as a wrathful communication from God visited upon the community as a consequence of its sinfulness. As such, it would call forth the ritual of prayer and rectification of the evil appropriate to purging the

[38] Miller, *The New England Mind: From Colony to Province*, p. 22.

[39] William Bradford, *Of Plymouth Plantation 1620–1647*, ed. Samuel Eliot Morison (Boston: Houghton Mifflin, 1912), p. 316.

underlying sin and therefore providing assurance of a continuation of the covenantal status. This interpretation, however, seems to overemphasize the degree to which crime was generally experienced as a community disaster on the scale of a drought or an Indian war. Winthrop's journal, for example, contains numerous references to murders, rapes, and other serious offenses with no indication that these events did or should evoke a collective repentance. The records of the General Court contain no orders for fasting or days of humiliation upon discovery of criminal harm. There was, at least in these early years, a strictly observed difference between sin and the afflictions that were its wages. The problem of individual crime was experienced on too small a scale to project the inference to the Puritan mind that there was serious underlying and causative sinfulness.

Later in the history of the Colony, says Miller, "the conception of the relation of society to the divine was unwittingly (and unintentionally) transformed into a thesis which positively reversed primitive doctrine."[40] The sinfulness of the society was no longer seen as a condition to be eradicated upon a vivid demonstration that it existed; rather, sin and corruption were themselves deemed visitations of the wrath of God. A pervasive and chronic state of spiritual impurity that could not be expiated replaced the sense of sin that had been experienced only at times and that even then could be removed through demonstrations of renewed adherence to covenant obligations. The "mental anguish" of the second and third generations in Massachusetts concerning their spiritual decline could no longer be measured by the external and objective phenomena of epidemic, war, famine, etc. These events were no longer the yardsticks for measuring culpability, and the expiating procedures became empty ritual and, in fact, devices for further reinforcing the pervasive sense of sin.

Miller attributes this change to the impact of a particular type of sermon, which he calls the "jeremiad" because its central theme was that the populace was being systematically taken to task for

---

[40] Miller, *The New England Mind: From Colony to Province*, p. 28.

its sins, a theme whose text frequently came from Jeremiah in the book of Isaiah.[41] In the course of collective assimilation of jeremiad thinking during the century, criminal acts acquire increased potential for signifying the perversity of the community, all the more so as the offenses take on the appearance of an epidemic directed at society at large. For this reason, it is of central importance to note Miller's statement that "an appearance of witchcraft among the afflictions of New England was from the beginning as much to be anticipated as Indian raids; by 1692 several instances had been encountered, and a more organized assault was altogether predictable."[42]

In view of Miller's thesis about the great significance of the jeremiad in the approximately thirty years from 1660 to 1692, the discovery of witches in the 1690's was more than predictable—but not at the beginning. It was, like the notion of the revocation of their charter, a shining confirmation of all that the Puritans had been led to believe for two generations concerning their abiding sinfulness and the dire calamities that would befall them as a consequence of that state. As more and more witches were discovered through the Salem investigations, the whole fiendish enterprise by the Devil and his workers must have become all the more understandable. Far from taking on the appearance of irrationality, the confessions of witch after witch would seem highly constructive and rational events in the life of the society. The presence of witches was clearly a calamity on the scale of epidemic or war. In this context how could anyone claim that the confessions sprang from madness? It followed logically from the collective fall from grace which the colonists had come to believe in. Significantly enough, the one person who did make such an assertion of madness, Thomas Brattle,[43] interpreted the Salem experience wholly outside of the traditional covenantal context, decrying the great stain on New England's reputation, not the

[41] *Ibid.*, pp. 27–39.
[42] *Ibid.*, p. 192.
[43] See Thomas Brattle's letter dated October 8, 1692, in Burr, *Narratives*, p. 173.

jeopardizing of her covenantal status.[44] Thus it seems that if the defense of insanity had a relatively small role in the witchcraft cases, it was not because of cruelty to mentally ill defendants. In the context of psychology and of New England covenantal history, the witchcraft that was charged and acknowledged was highly rational and far removed from the seventeenth-century concept of insanity.

[44] Miller, *The New England Mind: From Colony to Province*, pp. 196–97. The warning about impossible confessions was also made in England by Dr. John Webster, writing to several Justices of the Peace (see Kittredge, *Witchcraft in Old and New England*, p. 348). Webster's book was known to the Mathers (*ibid.*, p. 349), although the trustworthiness of the confession seems to have played no role in Increase Mather's *Cases of Conscience*, which Miller credits with putting a stop to the Salem trials (*The New England Mind: From Colony to Province*, pp. 198–200).

IX

THE LAW-SCIENCE RELATIONSHIP
THEN AND NOW

✠

Since this book's central concern is with law and science, it is fitting that it close with some mention of the problems lawyers now face, although it should be obvious from the previous chapters that there was no involvement of any sort of professional bar in the Massachusetts witchcraft cases. What we have observed instead is the influence of writers such as Michael Dalton, the administrative hand of men like John Winthrop, who had had some judicial experience, and the operation of a legal system that in many respects showed sophistication and justice. These latter virtues appeared often in the administration of the law and in its substantive content, both of which were in keeping with the best traditions of British due process and were in some details, such as the recording of the law in writing and the restricted use of capital punishment, well in advance of legal progress in the mother country. What this system of colonial justice might have been like if there had been a class of professional lawyers in New England can only be a matter of speculation. Given the low regard in which the English bar was held at the time, their presence might have been more of an impediment to the attainment of justice than anything else. But what is clear beyond speculation is that the administration of the law in the witchcraft prosecutions was related in some rather complex ways to the world of science and scientists, and these constitute the framework within which some important contemporary problems may be clarified.

The theme that runs through an examination of these cases is that the law was keeping very much in step with the scientific thought of the day. What emerges as the really difficult historical task is to identify any way in which law enforcement against witches actually conflicted with science. The neglect of post-mortem examinations certainly involved no disagreement between law and science, for, as the Rosseter report from Connecticut reveals, the demonological theory made the findings of a necropsy either irrelevant or confirmatory of a witch's involvement. There were no observations a doctor could record that would rule out the suspect's capability. This suggests, incidentally, that it is not our scientific sophistication that prevents us from taking witchcraft seriously now. We could term Elizabeth Kelley's terminal illness bronchial pneumonia or diphtheria, but the question of its spiritual causation would remain open. Science still remains the provider of only penultimate answers if we concede the potency of supernatural forces, as one may assume most persons who are orthodox in their religious beliefs would. It can be suggested that the principles of religion that were at the heart of the neglect of science in the death cases, far from being a demonstration of seventeenth-century fanaticism, were hardly more than an acknowledgment of the omnipotence of God that continues to be recognized today. The view that the universe of things is not merely a matter of insensible physical particles is commonly found among men of science, past and present. In one form or another, the scientist's rejection of a thoroughgoing materialism lent much support to the view that witches could cause the elements of nature to combine in fatal proportions.

So too there was no conflict when physicians were consulted during the course of a victim's illness. For the most part, it appears that purely medical procedures were followed, and, in a few cases, the inefficacy of these ministrations gave rise to suggestions of witchcraft. There was no infidelity to science even in these latter cases, for there was no doctrine or ethic that demanded limitation of the physician's role to an assessment of known symptoms, and widely held beliefs in some form of spiritualism supported a medical opinion that supernatural elements were at work.

But to say that the witchcraft trials had no anti-scientific elements tells much less than the whole story. The law-science amalgam in these cases reveals a great over-reliance on and uncritical use of science. An outstanding example is the matter of differential diagnosis. The validity or basis of a physician's pronouncement that his patient was a victim of witchcraft is nowhere questioned. Such judgments were readily accepted and given weight; there was none of the reluctance or hesitation inherent in Lawyer Dalton's *medical* observations. There was no inquiry into the problem of why, in some incurable and baffling physical illnesses, witchcraft appeared, and in others it did not. Why some physicians quickly reached the conclusion that a witch was involved in their patients' suffering, while other practitioners never ventured such an opinion, seemed to be a matter of no concern to anyone. The pervasive belief within the scientific community in spiritual control or influence over bodily functions, whether called an *élan* or a *Nishmath Chaim,* never appears openly as the premise for finding disease or death to have been supernaturally induced.

What tended to preclude a critical analysis of medical judgments was the universality and strength of the belief that people could and did behave as witches, causing the kind of harm that the expert opinions merely confirmed. But there is also the crucial question of who was to put forth the criticism, and where. The institutional ability to deal with medical judgments openly and on their merits was wholly lacking. It is true that several of the magistrates were personally involved in the world of science— through their membership in the Royal Society or otherwise—but the details of medical practice, both theoretical and practical, were not within their area of interest. Their scientific involvement was, in short, irrelevant to their capacity to judge the quality of diagnostic evaluations. Perhaps some of the witches who were themselves medical practitioners, such as Margaret Jones, had some sort of intellectual tools to voice a critique, but they were obviously not in a position to do so effectively. Furthermore, there was no requirement that the physician who was instrumental in launching a prosecution, as Dr. Griggs in Salem Village may have been in 1692, should testify at the actual trial. None of the validity testing that inheres in open judicial inquiry reached what may well have been the instigating factor of a case. The assumption that the victim was indeed suffering from witchly harm, with which the trial started, persisted throughout the proceedings, and no attempt was made to verify it by confronting and scrutinizing the underlying diagnostic judgment. There was thus neither the personnel nor the procedures for recognizing the limits of scientific expertise or for subjecting individual expert opinions to any sort of test.

Virtually everything said here about the uncritical acceptance of physicians' reports applies to the use of midwives as well. Their involvement in these cases ranks as the outstanding example of justice being blind when its eyes needed to be wide open. No doubt some evaluation of the women's reports could have been made, since standards of medical practice were evolving in the Colony by which their opinions might have been judged. It had been known for some time that substandard medical work was being carried on. There is even evidence of the prosecution of quacks, and, as has been suggested, some of the witchcraft cases may have been directed as much at controlling illegal medical practice as at *maleficium*. Yet no limitation seems to have been imposed on the use of the judgments of the searching women in the witchcraft cases. It may be recalled that in Connecticut a demand for "approbation" of physicians in these cases *was* made. It is not unlikely that in Massachusetts, too, some practitioners privately cautioned against relying strongly on the opinion of the women. If there were such reservations, however, little attention seems to have been paid to them. To some extent the use of a group of women rather than a single midwife did constitute an invitation to dissent, as well as an opportunity to obtain an opinion whose validity was vouched for by the unanimity of the panel or by the process of argument among its members when a consensus could not be reached. But for the most part this validity factor remained of only potential value to the judicial process, since there was no institutional way of bringing before the court the facts or opinions disputed among the women or of resolving issues raised by the accused's objection to the women's report. The judges seemed to consider that both they and the jury were incapable of dealing with these disagreements and that all that could be done, as the Nurse case illustrates, was to have the women take another look. But then, as before, the report was received by administrators of the law who were in no position to evaluate it.

In the areas where the law's use of scientific judgments should be characterized as an "under-use," the same problems appear. When the victim of an alleged witchcraft was dead, the theory of the Devil's working through natural causes was perhaps, as has been suggested, itself sufficient to make irrelevant post-mortem investigations. But this theory did not preclude medical ministrations while the victim lived, and it is likely that, if a cure could have been effected by the physician's manipulation of the right physical factors, a charge of witchcraft would have been extremely difficult, if not impossible, to maintain. Similarly, if autopsy in any case had revealed an obvious and familiar natural cause of death, it is unlikely that prosecution would have continued, in spite of demonological theory. There was, in other words, room to use scientific skills in far vaster areas than those in which they were in fact employed. But the local scientific community was not in a position to take the initiative in making a post-mortem examination; and no impetus to do this came from the legal system itself, in spite of the statutory framework that would have supported a broadened program of autopsies. Here was an instance in which the law might have demanded more from the scientists than they knew themselves capable of. In the absence of an awareness of the potential use of science on the part of those responsible for the legal system, the "apathy" of the scientists prevailed.

In the area of mental abnormality there was also statutory authority to do more than was actually done; dispensation for "distracted" persons was considered in only one witchcraft case. But even routine mental examinations in all cases probably would not have changed the outcome of a single trial, although this kind of guess can be made only most diffidently. All that can be said with assurance is that the law did not seek to apply what local skills there were in the field of psychodiagnosis in any case but that of Mary Glover. Perhaps it is important that of all the persons executed as witches in Massachusetts, Mrs. Glover was the only one who openly confessed her misdeeds. All of the pre-Salem offenders and all of those executed in that last series of prosecutions went to the gallows protesting their innocence to the end. The only sign of mental abnormality in the confession of a witch appeared in her case. There were, of course, other confessions—those of the Salem accused who realized that confession and repentance would allow witchcraft to go entirely unpunished. But this kind of absolution ritual was so deeply embedded in Puritan thought, even though the confessions were obviously meretricious, that there was no possibility of considering them to be a sign of insanity. If those who acknowledged their sin returned to a state of grace, so those who denied it were wicked and damned. It was almost entirely a question of one's status before divine judgment. The over-riding nature of this question tended to crowd out of consideration the matter of mental abnormality. There was, in short, such great cultural relativity involved in the use of physicians to diagnose the mental status of accused witches that the over-all result was a virtual neglect of the entire problem.

A serious question must now be raised concerning the justice of Massachusetts law administration in the cases. If justice involves bringing to bear in an informed way all that is relevant to the resolution of conflicts, then it must be said that it was injustice that characterized the use of science in the witchcraft controversy. To say this is not to point the finger of blame at those who were responsible for running the legal system or those who contributed their skills to the judicial process. There are a wealth of good reasons why a different pattern of law-science relations should not be expected. But, nonetheless, unjust it was, for the reason that relevant and available scientific knowledge was either not used at all or was accepted *in toto* and put to indiscriminate use.

Now that we think we know more of what science really is and have assigned a learned profession to the caretaking of justice, there is still a discomforting similarity to the kind of injustice that obtained three centuries ago. We do not try witches any more, although the exact reason why is not as obvious as one might expect. But more to the point is the question of what the administration of justice now does to bring in all the extralegal material that bears on the attainment of just results. One might advert initially to the process of judicial notice, whereby judges may take as proved anything that has become a recognized and accepted scientific fact. Obvious progress has also been achieved by allowing each side in a court case to call its own scientific expert and to crossexamine openly the scientists brought in by the other side. We know also that thinking about the problem of mental illness and legal responsibility is a great deal more sophisticated today. In some states a mental examination has become a routine matter in certain serious cases, and it would be highly unusual for a homicide trial to conclude without the testimony in court of a medical expert concerning his autopsy findings.

Yet all these advances leave more than a little to be desired. The ability of those charged with administering the law—lawyers and judges for the most part—to deal knowledgeably with scientific issues has not progressed very much beyond the days of the witchcraft trials. With full knowledge of the present and expanding importance of science in the legal process, we make no requirement that these professionals be anything but illiterates in science when they assume their responsibilities for the liberties, lives, and property of the populace. A student can come to law school with an undergraduate education that has no science in it at all, and law schools make no pretense at making up the deficit while he is in their charge. The brutal fact that even the best trained and most experienced scientists can differ among themselves on a precise question raised in court, thereby making the accuracy and sophistication of the judge's clarifying explanations to the jury crucial, has not prevented our elevating to the bench lawyers whose experience with science ended with a high-school biology course. The development of the adversary system and of the rule requiring a jury to limit its decision to the evidence openly presented to it provide the opportunity for skilled lawyers to bring forward and explain appropriate material from the world of science. But this reliance on the intellectual ability of an individual practitioner to teach himself a body of knowledge that is fast becoming more and more esoteric and specialized is surely a far from satisfactory means of dealing with the problem. The kind of critical evaluation of scientific material that this approach produces can be little more than minimal. The legal profession has the responsibility and the opportunity to serve justice better than this, but it is grossly lacking in the knowledge and training it needs to do so.

INDEX

Acquittals: examples of, 7, n. 13, 38; proportion of, 42–43

Alexander IV, Pope: on magicians, 15

Anatomy: criminal's body studied, 45–46; of female organs, 86–88; Galenic basis of, 55–56; as impetus for autopsies, 55–58; influence on English medicine, 56; legal authority to study, 45–46; and pathology, 56, 58; and Scientific Revolution, 55–56; taught by Giles Firman, 46; training in, 45

Astrology: in medical diagnosis, 85–86

Atheism: and disbelief in witches, 28–29

Autopsies: Connecticut report by Bryan Rossiter, 51–53, 110; demonological theory in Rossiter report, 110; Maryland cases, 47; Massachusetts cases, 48–49; modern use of, 113, 115. *See also* Medical theory; Physicians

Bacon, Francis: and new science, 32; on scholastic science, 3; and on science and religion, 33

Bible: Exodus proscribes witches, 12; magic in Joshua, 12

Bier right (ordeal by touch), 49

Bishop, Goody, 80

Boyle, Robert. *See* Religion

Brattle, Thomas: astronomer, 5, n. 6; on Cartesian philosophy in trials, 74; member of Royal Society, 57; non-covenantal basis of criticism by, 106–7; opposes search for Devil's marks, 78

Browne, Sir Thomas: known in Massachusetts, 61; on witches' use of natural forces, 60–61. *See also* Medical theory

Cartesianism. *See* Descartes, René

Confession: of Elizabeth Johnson, 93; and execution of witches, 114; by heretics, 17; by Mary Parsons, 42; number of, in Massachusetts, 106; untrustworthiness of, 107, n. 44; viewed as rational, 103; witches' use of, to escape punishment, 76

Connecticut: witch's marks found in autopsy, 51–53, 110

Covenant, Puritan: and defense of insanity, 103–7; effect of crime on, 104–5; and Thomas Brattle, 106–7. *See also* Insanity

Dalton, Michael: describes witch's marks, 77–78; influences trials, 109; on medical proof of witchcraft, 64–65; on medicine, 111

Descartes, René: attack on Newton by Cartesians, 71–72; influence on medical theory, 59; influence in trials, 74, 76; mechanism of, and trials, 4

Devil: as source of witchcraft, 13; superstition as pact with, 15; Wardwell's covenant with, 40

Devil's marks. *See* Witch's marks

Dudley, Joseph, 22

Designed by Arlene J. Sheer

*Composed in Intertype Garamond (text) and Monotype Garamont (display)
by Monotype Composition Company, Inc.*

Printed offset on 60-lb. P & S R by Universal Lithographers, Inc.

Bound in Columbia Fictionette by L. H. Jenkins, Inc.